Eccentric Britain

Eccentric Britain

A guide to Britain's bizarre buildings, peculiar places and offbeat events

Des Hannigan
Photography by Chris Coe

First published in 2004 by
New Holland Publishers (UK) Ltd
London • Cape Town • Sydney • Auckland
www.newhollandpublishers.com

Garfield House, 86–88 Edgware Road
London W2 2EA, United Kingdom
80 McKenzie Street, Cape Town 8001, South Africa
14 Aquatic Drive, Frenchs Forest, NSW 2086, Australia
218 Lake Road, Northcote, Auckland, New Zealand

10 9 8 7 6 5 4 3 2 1

ISBN 1 84330 731 6

Publishing Manager: Jo Hemmings
Project Editor: Camilla MacWhannell
Cover Design and Design: Alan Marshall & Gülen Shevki
Maps: William Smuts
Editor: Miren Lopategui
Production: Joan Woodroffe

Reproduction by Pica Digital Pte Ltd, Singapore
Printed and bound in Singapore by Kyodo Printing Co Pte Ltd

Page 1: ***A town crier in full cry.***
Page 2: ***Portmeirion, Gwynedd, Wales.***
Page 3: ***Interior of Highclere Castle, Hampshire.***
Opposite: ***Sword dancing at the Highland Games, Braemar, Aberdeenshire, Scotland.***
Page 7: ***The world famous Headington Shark, Oxfordshire.***
Page 155: ***Temple of Vaccinia, Berkeley, Gloucestershire.***
Page 160: ***The start/finishing line at Land's End, Cornwall.***

Contents

Introduction

'THE LUNATIC FRINGE WAGS THE UNDERDOG.'
H. L Mencken (1880–1956)

The British have always been slightly odd. It comes from living on an extremely crowded, yet incredibly diverse, offshore and off-centre island; one that's big enough to have influenced every corner of the world, yet small enough to be recognizably insular – unique, fascinating and delightfully eccentric.

The word 'eccentric' has its roots in the ancient Greek *ekkentros*, meaning 'off-centre' – a phrase that is deeply satisfying to the independent soul. *The Oxford English Dictionary* defines eccentric as: 'not concentric with another circle, having little in common; regulated by no central control; irregular, anomalous; capricious; (of person, etc.) odd, whimsical.'

The British fit the odd and whimsical bill perfectly. The very fact of being British suggests eccentricity for many people, who agree with Noël Coward that 'Mad dogs and Englishmen [and women] go out in the midday sun'. There is unquestionably something in the British psyche – some intangible, precious spirit – that happily eschews the norm, rejects the conventional and cherishes individuality. It is, perhaps, a reaction to the crowded nature of the island; a cherishing of individuality, because there's not much elbow-room.

In spite of this, few Britons would openly claim to be eccentric. Most British people display a general fondness towards harmlessly odd behaviour; but the British are also famously private and are easily embarrassed. The entertainer Julian Clary, who has managed to conflate genuine eccentricity with exhibitionism, once pointed out that while the English may like eccentrics, they don't want them living next door.

Eccentricity is written across the face of Britain. From the spectacular Land's End, at the far south-western tip of England, to Scotland's lonely northern outpost of John o' Groats, it's only around 1300 kilometres (800 miles) as the crow flies; but crammed into that small compass is a huge variety of landscapes, cities, towns, villages, neighbourhoods, religions, traditions, dialects, attitudes and individuals, a magic mix that has produced a cornucopia of eccentricity. From north to south and from east to west, the dramatic and magnificent story of Britain has always been leavened by the quirky, the bizarre, the irreverent and the downright dotty.

This book offers an intriguing – and sometimes tongue-in-cheek – journey through British eccentricity via a succession of gloriously useless follies, stately homes full of weird features and odd artefacts, hills and headlands with magical powers and buildings that have gone engagingly awry. Scattered among this banquet of the bizarre are colourful events that honour ancient ceremonies or promote wildly illogical sports and pastimes. Daft days out, crazy carnivals, fantastic festivals... they're all here in bucket-loads. And behind this effulgence of eccentricity is a marvellous roll-call of eccentric individuals.

Eccentric Britain explores every quirky aspect of the nation; from a nude hiker setting off on the long walk from Land's End to John o' Groats to the even more outrageous exposé of Dorset's Cerne Abbas giant, outlined in chalk on a green hillside in all its rude glory; from London's Pearly Kings and Queens to the World Conker Championships in Northamptonshire; from chasing cheeses down helter-skelter hillsides in Gloucestershire to a 'helter-skelter' house in Norfolk.

When it comes to mad-hattery, Wales and Scotland are not far behind England. Where else but Wales would

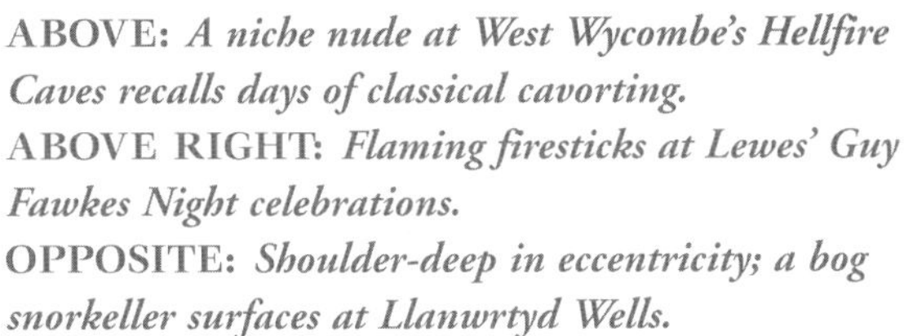

ABOVE: ***A niche nude at West Wycombe's Hellfire Caves recalls days of classical cavorting.***
ABOVE RIGHT: ***Flaming firesticks at Lewes' Guy Fawkes Night celebrations.***
OPPOSITE: ***Shoulder-deep in eccentricity; a bog snorkeller surfaces at Llanwrtyd Wells.***

you find people eager to submerge themselves for fun in a freezing bog? Where else can you hop on to a train that hauls itself to the top of one of the highest mountains in Britain, then comes all the way back down again? And in Scotland, you'll find a pineapple-shaped house, the Loch Ness Monster, the world's best worst poet and deep-fried Mars Bars.

All those crazy British ceremonies and customs that date back centuries – the cheese-rollings, the straw bears, hobby horses and Morris dances – have their modern counterparts in nettle-eating championships and lawnmower racing, while more and more ancient ceremonies and festivals that have been in abeyance for centuries are being enthusiastically resurrected. All those bizarre buildings and follies are mirrored in marvellous modern edifices, such as the London Eye and the Angel of the North. All those wild-eyed dreamers and distracted geniuses of history have their inheritors in every quiet corner of Britain.

In spite of everything, this offshore, off-centre, happily odd island is, in the end, the very centre of the eccentric.

Cornwall & Devon

In England's far western counties of Cornwall and Devon eccentricity is given a head start by the region's potent sense of unexplained forces that encourage the creative, the colourful and the downright quirky at every turn. From the golden granite cliffs and smugglers' coves of Cornwall to the misty wilderness of Devon's Dartmoor, this is a world of exquisite natural beauty; a world where the line between myth and reality is often endearingly blurred, where legends are larger than life and where summer festivals resonate with rumbustious folk memories and the echoes of a pagan past. Round every corner you'll find madcap May Days, inexplicable memorials, mermaids, merry maids and an exhilarating mélange of history and tradition, legend and lore, freedom and free expression.

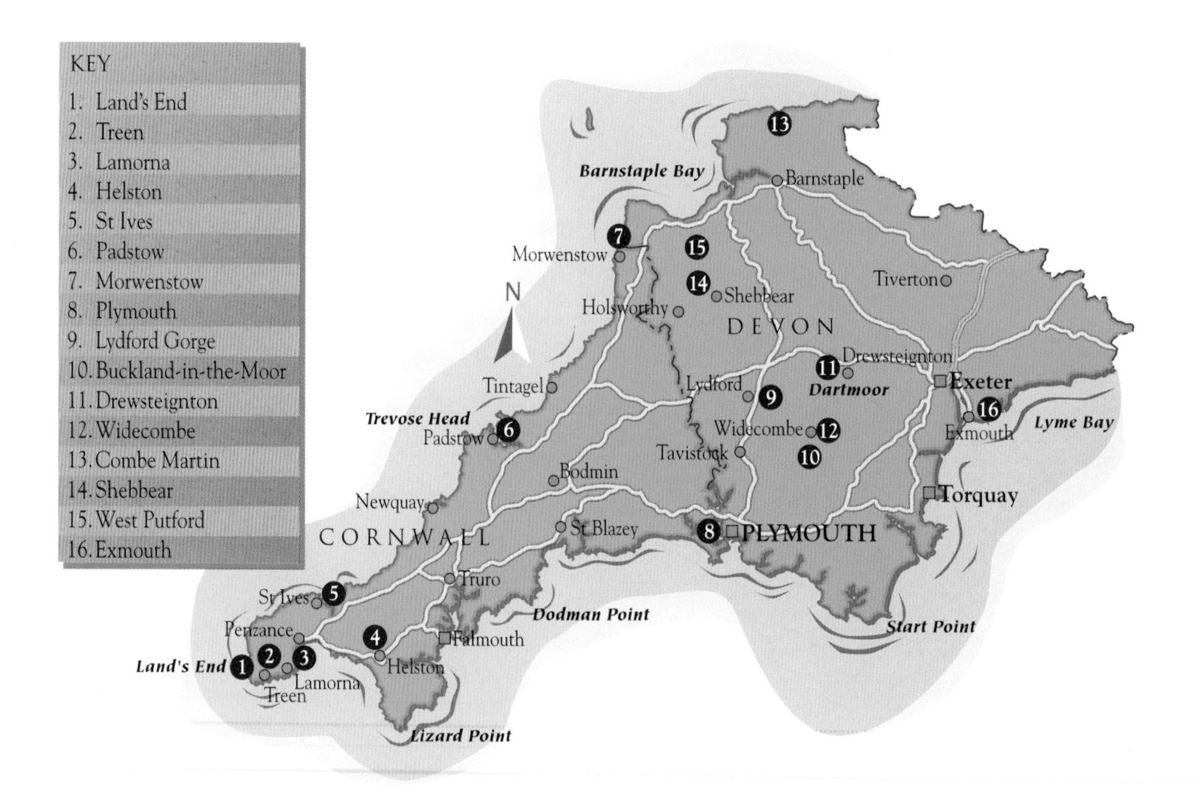

CONTEMPORARY FINE ART
CURIOS
O'NEILL

May Days, Merry Maids, Rones, Stones & Ancient Bones

Making Ends Meet

Land's End, Cornwall

They've done it on foot, on bicycles, in vintage cars, on horseback, in fancy dress – and with no dress at all. That's the wonderful cast of Britain's maddest marathon, the 1407-kilometre (875-mile) trip through the length of Britain, from Land's End in Cornwall to John o' Groats at the northern tip of Scotland – or vice versa.

There's even an official End to End Club for the large number of people who have made the trip during the past 50 years or so. Most do it for charity, some do it for publicity, but none has expressed such naked eccentricity as 44-year-old Steve Gough, who set off from Land's End in June 2003, stark naked apart from a rucksack, boots, hat and watch. Mr Gough was already notorious as a one-man campaigner for what he called 'public expression' and 'personal freedom' through promoting a healthy body image. He had made several court appearances and once turned up for an interview on a BBC John Peel radio show, stark naked, except for a name badge.

LEFT: ***The redoubtable Steve Gough, ever prominent in his determined campaign for public expression and freedom of the person, is pictured on the long, hot road from Land's End to John o' Groats.***

PREVIOUS PAGE: ***'Sumer is icumen in' at Padstow's Madcap May Day when the picturesque Cornish village becomes even more colourful and lively.***

Soon after leaving on his End to End adventure, Steve was arrested and charged with 'causing public alarm'. He was soon released, with yet another caution, and headed nakedly north. Over the next few weeks, reports of naked hikers poured in from various parts of England and even serious newspapers sent reporters out to strip off and hike. But there was no army of 'boots only' hikers out there; no new nude craze was sweeping the country. Most of the sightings were of the irrepressible Mr Gough, carrying a torch – or words to that effect – for public expression. Five months, 15 arrests and 140 nights in prison after leaving a sunny Land's End, Steve Gough reached a bitterly cold John o' Groats. He quickly donned some clothes, but remained as bare-faced as ever about his crusade for the naked truth.

'THE WORST REACTION I GOT WAS WHEN I SAID HELLO TO SOMEONE AND THEY DID NOT ANSWER.'

Naked walker Steve Gough passing comment on the Great British attitude to passing nudity.

THE LOGAN ROCK & ROLL

Treen, Cornwall

Faith may not actually move mountains, but in 19th-century Cornwall a young naval officer once toppled a 70-tonne (77-ton) rock from its perilous perch – and then had to put it back again.

The rock is known as Logan Rock and lies among a fabulous pile of wind-polished boulders that crowns a rugged sea promontory near the beautiful beach of Porthcurno, between Penzance and Land's End. It is named after the Cornish word *loggan*, which means 'to rock', because it was once so finely balanced that you could make it vibrate by pushing a certain spot with just one finger. It was said to be impossible to dislodge the rock – a challenge that roused a spirited young naval lieutenant, Hugh Goldsmith, a distant relative of the 18th-century dramatist, Oliver Goldsmith. One day in 1824, young Hugh, with a dozen sailors and a pile of crowbars, hopped ashore from a naval cutter that was moored in the vicinity and toppled the mighty Logan Rock from its perch.

The rock fell only a few feet, but there was a furious response throughout Cornwall at what was seen as rank vandalism. A contrite Goldsmith undertook to replace the stone at his own expense. It took several months to assemble blocks, chains, capstans, ropes and huge wooden shear legs, with which Goldsmith and teams of sailors and local workmen took four days to haul the mighty Logan Rock back on to its throne in front of an audience of thousands.

BELOW: *Looking across Porthcurno Bay to the rugged headland of Treryn Dinas (Treen Castle), cradle of the rock 'n' rolling Logan Rock.*

ABOVE: *Give a stone a great big hug. Rosemodress Circle, aka The Merry Maidens, near Lamorna. Ancient ceremonial site or legendary lasses?*

The feat cost £130 8s. 6d., a large amount for the time. The account bill is still on display at the Logan Rock Inn in the nearby village of Treen. It shows an inordinate amount of beer was supplied for the workers. It's thirsty work when you rock and roll.

CLOSING THE CIRCLE
Lamorna, Cornwall

Free the spirit! Hug a rock! seems to be the inspiration for certain happy people who hunt out the mysterious standing stones and stone circles of Britain's prehistoric monuments.

Archaeologists say that such structures were probably ceremonial sites or gathering places for social and commercial events, thousands of years ago. Other people say they were aligned with the sun, moon and stars and that they possessed magic properties of healing and prediction. Modern devotees of these latter theories still gather at many of Britain's ancient sites on midsummer midnights, and on other 'sacred' days, to enact what they imagine were the rituals of the ancients. They hug the stones for comfort and for inspiration and some even get married at their 'sacred' centres.

One of Cornwall's most famous stone circles stands in a roadside field near Lamorna, to the west of Penzance. Its official name is Rosemodress Circle, but it's better known as The Merry Maidens after popular 'scare' stories of later Christian times that warned of young girls being turned to stone for dancing on the Sabbath.

In the face of all this excited attention the stones have maintained a stony silence. They did so even in the face of a notorious event in the 1980s when a well-known chocolate manufacturer ran a series of adverts featuring clues to the whereabouts of a bejewelled 'egg' buried somewhere in Britain and worth several thousand pounds. Frantic searching ensued, with manic egg-hunters even digging up people's gardens and, in one case, a private grave-site. The Merry Maidens did not escape and one morning the farmer who owned the field found a devoted egg-hunter digging up one of the stones, convinced that the 'golden egg' lay beneath.

Ancient monuments such as The Merry Maidens are protected by law from such vandalism, of course. Disturb them and you may even be turned to stone yourself...

Helston Furry Dance

Helston, Cornwall

There's dancing in the streets of the attractive town of Helston every 8th May, when impeccably dressed couples – ladies in sumptuous hats and ball gowns, gents in top hats and tails – waltz through the town in a sort of decorous conga.

This is the famous Helston Flora, or Furry Dance, a celebration that probably derives from pagan fertility ceremonies that were later appropriated by Christianity, their often riotous rituals made respectable. The name Flora might represent the Roman goddess of flowers. But Furry? Who knows? It might just have been the way the rich and melodious Cornish accent sorted out the rather bland word 'flora' many years ago

Helston is said to have got its name from a sizzling 'hell stone' dropped accidentally by the Devil – or a dragon – out for a leisurely flight. Cool logic suggests that a meteorite may have dropped on an original small settlement in the very distant past, and Helston's name probably derives from a Cornish word for 'sunny meadow'. It's a devil of a good story all the same and an alternative explanation for Helston Flora is that local people were said to have been so relieved at surviving this fire-and-brimstone attack that they danced in and out of each other's houses.

Flora Day was banned during the 19th century as still being too close to the pagan bone and because 'riotous' behaviour was still evident during the celebrations. Reinstated early in the 20th century, it is now the high point of Helston's year and is a colourful and enjoyable event as invited couples dance through the crowded and flower-bedecked streets, through people's gardens and in the front door and out the back door of houses, to the repetitive, but catchy tune of 'The Helston Flora Dance'.

ABOVE: *Knill's Steeple above St Ives. Failed Cornish space rocket, eccentric mausoleum, or useful landmark for smugglers?*

Knill's steeple

St Ives, Cornwall

High above the famous Cornish holiday resort of St Ives, on Worvas Hill, stands Knill's Steeple – a sombre granite pyramid, simple, unadorned, yet utterly intriguing. Is it an ancient trigonometry point? A failed Cornish space rocket, as some locals will slyly tell you? Or a bid to make Worvas Hill higher than it is?

The truth is even stranger. This is the mausoleum of an 18th-century mayor of St Ives, John Knill – a man who seems to have mixed classic eccentricity with immense cleverness. Knill was also the official Collector of Customs at a time when smuggling was a way of life in Cornwall. He seems to have made a great deal of money and it was alleged that while he was mayor, smuggling prospered and few smugglers were ever caught.

In 1797, Knill paid for the building on Worvas Hill of a 15-metre (49-foot) tall mausoleum in which his body was to be placed after death. He also bequeathed money to pay for a strange ceremony in which, every five years, ten girls under the age of ten should dance round the mausoleum to the playing of a fiddle. The children had to be daughters of seamen, fishermen or tin miners and two venerable widows of the same social background were to attend them. There is no explanation of why the details of the ceremony were so precise.

John Knill died in 1811, aged 77. Ironically he was buried in London; but the strange ceremony he conjured out of nowhere has been celebrated ever since and is today one of Cornwall's most famous events. The next Knill Celebration is in 2006.

ABOVE: ***The stuff of delicious nightmare: Padstow's 'Obby 'Oss drives the dance on May Day.***
BELOW: ***Flags, flowers and fun on Padstow's May Day.***

A Madcap May Day

Padstow, Cornwall

Summer comes in with a flourish at the Cornish port of Padstow, every madcap May Day. That's when the town celebrates the Obby Oss Ceremony, an ancient festival aimed at welcoming the summer and ensuring a fruitful harvest. On the day, two hooped 'masks', painted and plumed and representing symbolic horses with trailing black skirts, are paraded through the town from dawn to dusk. Musicians accompany the entire cavalcade playing the repetitive but haunting tune, 'The Obby Oss May Song'. The event turns

Padstow's narrow streets and harbourside into a riotous festival of colour, noise and general horsing about.

For days beforehand Padstow is decked out with flags and greenery and on May Day morning, a blue Oss, also known as the Peace Oss, and a Red, or Old, Oss, compete for attention. Both have their own 'stables' in local pubs, and each has a team of devoted attendants, dressed in white. The Osses are led by a Teazer wielding a painted club.

The Osses are manipulated by a team member who, hidden out of sight beneath the black cloth of the hoop and skirts, ensures that the Osses follow a wild and swooping dance through the narrow streets. Operators change places at regular intervals, usually outside one of Padstow's many pubs, where everyone pauses for breath and beer.

ABOVE: ***Morwenstow Vicarage, with its chimneys masquerading as eccentric reproductions of church and college towers and a gravestone.***

Each Obby Oss chases any man who gets near it, and tries to drag young women (who are not always unwilling) beneath its black skirt. The earthiness and sexual overtones are obvious and the festival was banned during the morally rigorous 19th century because it was seen by Church and authorities as being too pagan and 'licentious'. The festival was reinstated early last century, however, and it has galvanized the town's May Day ever since.

If you ever get the chance to be in Padstow on May Day, it's a wonderful experience; but don't expect a quiet time as, in the words of the May Day song, 'Sumer is icumen in...'

The Morbidly Merry Vicar

Morwenstow, Cornwall

Not everyone takes their pet pig for a walk or dresses as a mermaid; but these were just two of the fascinating habits of the Reverend Robert Stephen Hawker, one of the greatest of 19th-century English eccentrics and a man of genius and immense humanity.

Hawker was well suited to the gaunt sea cliffs, gloomy woods, roaring seas and ghostly legends of North Cornwall's Morwenstow parish, where he was vicar from 1834 to 1874. For a start, he built a series of quirky chimneys onto his vicarage: three were in the shape of favourite church towers, one was a copy of the tower of an Oxford college, and one an exact replica of his mother's grave.

Hawker was devoted to his parishioners, most of whom were poor farmers and fishermen. His humanity extended to making often desperate efforts to save shipwrecked sailors on Morwenstow's savage coast. Few sailors survived being wrecked against the awesome cliffs, but Hawker made it his duty to give them a decent burial, at least – the graveyard at Morwenstow pays homage to the drowned of numerous wrecks. Hawker scoured the desolate shoreline, after a shipwreck, in search of often gruesome remains. The story goes that he dragooned reluctant parishioners into helping him, often dosing them with gin to overcome their revulsion and superstition.

Hawker is said to have dosed himself with other substances, too. He certainly smoked opium, as per the 'Romantic' fashion of poet Samuel Taylor Coleridge and essayist Thomas de Quincey. At the tiny Hawker's Hut – a driftwood shack now in the care of the National Trust – that nestles just below the cliff edge near Morwenstow vicarage, Parson Hawker wrote and meditated, often under the influence. He once dressed as a mermaid and ensconced himself on a rock at low tide on the beach at the nearby seaside village of Bude. The prank backfired, however, and Hawker beat a hasty retreat when a curious fisherman arrived waving a blunderbuss. Hawker also took his pet pig, Gyp, for long walks, and once excommunicated a cat for catching a mouse on a Sunday. And why not...?

DEAD DRAWER

Plymouth, Devon

Eccentricity was a way of life for the Plymouth-based painter Robert Lenkiewicz, a man of Falstaffian girth and an epic spirit to go with it; he hid the embalmed body of a tramp in his studio for 17 years.

Robert Lenkiewicz was born in London in 1941 and even at the age of nine had produced skilful paintings using brushes made from his own hair. He studied at prestigious London art schools and during the 1960s, settled in Plymouth's dockside area, The Barbican.

Lenkiewicz's vigorous portrayal of the seamier side of life transformed the images of his often broken subjects – tramps, beggars and derelicts – into luminous figurative paintings. Lenkiewicz loved women lasciviously and his portrayal of the female form was always voluptuous, arch and titillating. He loved nothing better than the mischievous teasing of establishment figures; a huge mural that he painted on the side of a building in The Barbican featured a lively cornucopia of gambolling nudes, many of whom were recognizable local establishment figures.

But Lenkiewicz's most eccentric action was the sequestering of the corpse of a homeless man, Edwin Mackenzie, who was said to live in a barrel and was, perhaps, inevitably nicknamed after the ancient Greek philosopher Diogenes, an original eccentric of the highest order who, according to legend, lived in a tub. (The original Diogenes was once visited by an admiring

LEFT: ***A classic Robert Lenkiewicz mural in Plymouth depicts much bare flesh and a number of people as they probably never wanted to see themselves.***

Alexander the Great, who offered him whatever he wanted in life. 'Step aside, Your Greatness,' Diogenes said. 'You're blocking out the sun.')

When Edwin Mackenzie died in 1985 Lenkiewicz had the body embalmed and then hid it from council officers who searched the artist's rambling studio. Of the dead Diogenes there was no sign, but they found a grinning Lenkiewicz, lying in a drawer. Needless to say, the mummified remains of Diogenes were found in the same drawer after Lenkiewicz's death, aged 60, in 2002.

The Gruesome Gubbinses

Lydford Gorge, Devon

Devon's magnificent wilderness of Dartmoor is awash with monstrous myth and legend, often based on monstrous fact. One such legend centres on the eccentric, and infamous Gubbins family, a tribe of allegedly half-human creatures whose den lay on the western edges of northern Dartmoor at the heart of the dramatic Lydford Gorge, through which the River Lyd roars and foams in spectacular cataracts.

The Gubbinses did exist and are said to have settled in the area during the 15th century. For over 200 years generations of this wild, extraordinary family terrorized Dartmoor, stealing sheep and cattle, plundering farmsteads, and robbing and kidnapping travellers. Hideous myths attached to them, including the scurrilous allegations that they were cannibals and that they were incestuous.

Some sources argue that the Gubbinses were originally poor but respectable farmers who were law-abiding, loyal supporters of King Charles I. When a King's Officer seduced and betrayed a favourite Gubbins daughter, the family took revenge by killing the perpetrator, an act that led to all bearers of the Gubbins name being outlawed and stripped of their land and possessions.

In response the Gubbinses robbed and plundered to survive and were said to have become so tough and adept that they could outrun on foot horsemen sent to hunt them down and could lose hounds in the deep bogs and boulder fields of Dartmoor. No one dared venture into the heart of Lydford Gorge to tackle them. In later years the tribe declined, it was said through disease and interbreeding.

RIGHT: ***The White Lady waterfall is one of the spectacular features in Lydford Gorge, where the Gubbinses are said to have gorged themselves on human flesh.***

Today, the beautiful Lydford Gorge is in the care of the National Trust. The gorge is open to visitors who can follow a protected walkway to where the River Lyd tumbles between narrow walls at the spectacular Devil's Cauldron. You can be fairly confident that no hungry Gubbinses still lurk in the dense undergrowth. But then again...

God's Graffiti

Buckland-in-the-Moor, Devon

Down in deepest Devon, near the beautiful Dartmoor village of Buckland-in-the-Moor, is a spectacular example of religious graffiti. It takes the form of the wording of the Ten Commandments, skilfully carved on large slate stones, and was the inspiration of William Whitley, a local man of fierce religious conviction.

In the 1920s, Whitley opposed the introduction of a revised version of *The English Prayer Book*, because of alleged Anglo-Catholic influences in the text. The revised version had the support of just about everyone in the Church of England and its passage through the

ABOVE: ***The Ten Commandments Stones on lonely Buckland Beacon.***
OPPOSITE: ***The Mother of all church clocks on the tower of St John the Baptist church.***

British Parliament seemed assured. However, there was one other influential dissenter, the Home Secretary of the day, Sir William Joynson-Hicks. Like Whitley, Joynson-Hicks was implacably opposed to the new prayer book and he persuaded the House of Commons to reject its publication.

William Whitley was jubilant at what he saw as a reversal of 'Popish' influences and to celebrate the triumph commissioned William Clement, a stonemason from Exeter to carve the Ten Commandments on 'tablets of stone' on the nearby hilltop of Buckland Beacon.

The job took Clement 40 days (his nights were spent in an old cowshed) and Mr Whitley nicknamed him Moses. Clement's monumental work remains on the glossy black boulders on the lonely moor, but it was a Pyrrhic victory for William Whitley and fellow dissenters. The English bishops ignored the House of Commons ruling and simply introduced at a later date, illegally, the new version of the Prayer Book. It survives to this day; but so do the marvellous Ten Commandments stones.

The eccentric Mr Whitley is also responsible for the fascinating clock face on the lovely little church of St John the Baptist at the heart of Buckland-in-the-Moor. Your eyes won't deceive you. Instead of numerals encircling the clock face, there stands the 12-letter inscription 'My Dear Mother'.

To the Manor and the Manner Born

Drewsteignton, Devon

Every British home is a castle, according to the proud saying, whether it's a one-roomed shack or a royal palace. Few people still live in castles, however, and no one builds them anymore.

Sir Julius Drewe, a wealthy tea importer who founded the Home and Colonial Stores in the 1880s, did build himself a castle, the last to be built in England, above the beautiful wooded River Teign. Whether this grand gesture reflected an endearing eccentricity – Drewe was convinced he was directly descended from a 12th-century Norman baron called Drogo de Teign and called his 'ancestral' pile Castle

A Grey Mare's Tale

Widecombe, Devon

Dartmoor's annual Widecombe Fair takes place on the second Tuesday in September each year. The event dates back at least a couple of hundred years and is like most rural fairs; but its association with a world-famous song has turned Widecombe into a major tourist honeypot, although the village's beautiful location draws the crowds anyway. Widecombe Fair and the famous song have a grip on the public imagination. The first verse alone is recognizable world wide:

Tom Pearce, Tom Pearce, lend me your grey mare,
All along, down along, out along lee.
For I want to go to Widecombe Fair,
Wi' Bill Brewer, Jan Stewer, Peter Gurney,
Peter Davy, Dan'l Whiddon. Harry Hawk,
Old Uncle Tom Cobley and all.

It is this litany of dyed-in-the-wool Devon names that conjures up a vivid picture of rural Britain, linked to the slightly raffish character of the eight horsemen who commandeered Tom Pearce's old mare to carry them to Widecombe. That the poor, overburdened mare 'took sick and died' on the way home is hardly surprising. It strikes a sympathetic chord in today's world, in which the unremarkable equivalent would be borrowing someone's old van.

Today's Widecombe Fair has it's own re-enactment of the story, complete with Uncle Tom Cobley and Tom Pearce's mare to go with a marvellous mix of sheep trial, tug-o'-war, rural crafts and rich Devon food. At the end of the day everyone heads home in cars, coaches and on horseback, while the alleged ghosts of the Grey Mare's original merry crew wander off across the dusky moor – singing a peculiar old song.

Drogo – or was simply the happy indulgence of a very rich man, is irrelevant. Sir Julius has left a fabulous legacy for the rest of us to enjoy, as his castle is now in the care of the National Trust.

Castle Drogo might easily have become a magnificent folly. It was designed by the brilliant architect Edwin Lutyens, who first submitted plans for a building of such epic proportions that not even Julius Drewe's fortune could measure up to the projected expense.

The plans were reduced by a third, yet construction took 20 years. The result is still awesome; Castle Drogo is a vision of crusader towers and massive curtain walls. There are medieval and Tudor features aplenty, from the uncluttered granite façades and authentic portcullis, to mullioned windows, crenellated battlements and octagonal turrets, while the interior is splendid and austere; granite lending itself satisfyingly to the medieval style.

Long Road to Rone

Combe Martin, Devon

The village of Combe Martin, on the beautiful north coast of Devon, has a main street that is over 2 kilometres (a mile) in length. Part way along is a fascinating building, known as the Pack of Cards Inn, which dates from the early 17th century and was built by a successful gambler in celebration of a big win at cards. The Pack has 52 windows and four floors, each one with 13 doors.

Apart from all this purely structural eccentricity, Combe Martin stages a very odd but fascinating annual ceremony in late May, known as Hunting the Earl of Rone. Like many other May-time festivals, the event features a large hobby horse with snapping jaws; add to this a real donkey, a traditional jester wielding a broom, a troop of red-coated soldiers carrying mock muskets, and a wonderful crowd of drummers, accordion players and assorted musicians, and you have an event that can truly be described as eccentric.

Central to the ceremony is the symbolic figure of the unfortunate Earl of Rone, thought to represent the Earl of Tyrone, who escaped from Ireland after being involved in rebellion against British rule in 1607 and was shipwrecked on the North Devon coast. The Earl

RIGHT: ***Building for posterity. Castle Drogo above the wooded valley of the River Teign on Dartmoor was Sir Julius Drewe's homage to his dreams of Norman ancestry and was the last 'castle' to be built in England.***

was captured, the story goes, and taken to the local jail, bound back-to-front on a donkey, while his captors banged pots and pans together in a traditional form of ridicule. The event was probably later merged with traditional May festivals, but was suspended during the 1830s because of religious disapproval of the 'licencious [sic] drunkenness' of those taking part.

The Hunting was reinstated in the year 2000 and lasts for several days, with participants looking for the elusive earl in the surrounding woods and along the cliff tops. He's eventually captured and is then dressed in sackcloth and, with a dramatic mask hiding his face, is mounted on the donkey. To the noisy accompaniment of blank musket shots, drum beats and lively music, the earl is then taken down to the sea – and thrown in. Then everyone, including the earl, retires to the village pubs for a little bit of license...

ABOVE: ***Hot roast tonight at the Devil's Stone Inn, Shebbear.*** **BELOW:** ***Shebbear's Devil's Stone lies innocuously on the ground.***

Stoning the Devil

Shebbear, Devon

The Devil and his cronies seem to be afflicted with butter fingers – if the number of 'hell stones' and 'Devil's rocks' that litter rural Britain are anything to go by; all of them dropped from a great height by some satanic figure on a short-haul flight.

The Devil's Stone that lies outside St Michael's Church in the idyllic North Devon village of Shebbear weighs just under one tonne and according to legend

was dropped by the Archangel Lucifer on his descent from heaven to hell. Why Lucifer was carrying the stone is anyone's guess, but it was probably very hot.

Somewhere along the line of legend, the good villagers of Shebbear were warned that if they did not move the stone at least once a year, disaster would strike the district. Consequently, on 5th November, Guy Fawkes Night, every year the accomplished bell-ringers of St Michael's ring a purposefully cacophonous peal on the church bells, probably aimed at confusing any devils lurking in the undergrowth. The bell-ringers then emerge on to the little village green where the stone lies and solemnly turn the stone over with crowbars. They then return to the church, where they ring a second, more tuneful, celebratory peal.

In the 1930s, a well-meaning vicar decided that blessing the stone was a far more Christian thing to do, but old habits, and superstitions, die hard and local unease at this tempting of fiery fate was such that the custom of physically turning the stone was reinstated.

St Michael's Church is well-guarded against Satan and all his works. The church's Norman south doorway is carved with elaborate beak heads that are ferocious enough to stop any old devil in its tracks.

ABOVE: *Fancy a game of chess? A gnomic gathering at West Putford's Gnome Reserve proves that gnomes lead a checkered life.*

Giving a Gnome a Home

West Putford, Devon

Give a gnome a home in your garden and you may earn the ridicule of modern gardeners and gardening celebrities. Gardens are fashion statements these days and the garden gnome is not quite cat walk. They're even banned from taking part in Britain's Royal Horticultural Society's Chelsea Flower Show, the *haute couture* event of the gardening world.

Yet most people have an amused fondness for these kitschy little creatures and at West Putford in Devon, the devoted Ann Atkin has created a marvellous Gnome Reserve and Wildflower Garden where over 1000 gnomes happily populate two-and-a-half acres of rustic paradise.

The garden gnome as ornament may well be a suburban descendant of classical ornamentation, a pop version of the gargoyle liberated. The first recorded

appearance of a garden gnome in England was on the 19th-century estate of the eccentric Charles Isham, 10th Baronet of Lamport Hall in Northamptonshire. Isham created an ornamental garden in the already substantial grounds of his handsome home and filled it with all manner of bizarre objects, including a little tribe of imported gnome statues from Germany. A solitary survivor of the Lamport Victorian gnomes was recently discovered and now holds the distinguished title of the World's Oldest Gnome. It was not, however, until the mid-20th century that the gnome as garden object became a truly popular icon, facilitated by the use of concrete for mass production.

Ann Atkin argues persuasively for the garden gnome as therapy and finds that sceptics and scoffers who visit her Gnome Reserve nearly always leave enchanted. She supplies pointy hats for all visitors to wear. A good point; it brings every generation happily down to gnome levels. Atkin's Gnome Reserve has even been entered as a candidate for the famous Turner Art Prize, although it never quite made it alongside artist Damien Hirst's dead cow in formaldehyde. Some may wonder why not...

Squaring the Circle

Exmouth, Devon

The sun shines a lot at Exmouth on Devon's south-facing coast and for two extraordinary 18th-century sisters, Jane and Mary Parminter, it was this that inspired their creation of A la Ronde, a delightful 16-sided house that is now one of the National Trust's most endearing properties.

There is nothing 'folly-ish' about A la Ronde. It was built to the Parminter sisters' design after their ten years of travelling throughout mainland Europe. All 16 sides of this singular building have generous windows and even the wall junctions have delightful triangular

OPPOSITE: ***Gnomes-on-wheels at West Putford's Gnome Reserve head for the checkered flag in their checkered life.***

ABOVE: ***The enchanting A La Ronde at Exmouth, dream home of the Parminter sisters, who kept the sun in sight at every turn.***

lights. For purists, of course, the name A la Ronde does not quite ring true, the house being an octagon rather than a 'ronde'. But the phrase had more to do with the all-encircling light so beloved of the Parminters. Their purpose was to ensure that the interior of the house would enjoy maximum sunlight from dawn to dusk. The bedroom window, for example, was east-facing, to start the day with a smile.

The Parminter sisters were already well-used to the sun. They had been born in Lisbon, Portugal, and their European travels took them to the Mediterranean, where their inspiration for A la Ronde is said to have come from many visits to Byzantine churches such as Verona's Church of San Vitale.

San Vitale has a distinctive octagonal nave and a 16-sided exterior, and it was with this in mind that the Parminters commissioned their own Byzantine building. A la Ronde originally had a thatched roof and was probably more basic than today's elegant building. It was known locally as the South Sea Island Hut, but during the 19th century acquired a red-tiled roof with dormer windows. Some of the house's original eccentric charm may have been lost, but A la Ronde remains a magical building, not least because of its most exotic and startling feature, the Shell Gallery, created by the Parminters as a life's work. Jane and Mary spent much painstaking time embedding tens of thousands of sea shells, pottery fragments, small stones and feathers into the upper walls and roof to create a highly unusual gallery that is now nationally famous.

Somerset, Dorset & Wiltshire

The quintessential English counties of Somerset, Dorset and Wiltshire are far less dramatic in terms of landscape than Cornwall and Devon, yet their long history of human settlement gives them the edge over many places when it comes to rich traditions and to a deep-seated sense of English identity. On the limestone hills of Dorset, on Somerset's tawny Exmoor, on Wiltshire's rolling downs, the people of Britain have settled since time immemorial. This is a land where the hard facts of history blur into myth and legend, where ancient monuments and sophisticated Gothic cathedrals rub shoulders with devotion to mythical kings and giants – where life is led at a gently reflective pace, and where the unexpected becomes the norm.

Clocks, Shocks, Stings and Things

A Lifelike but Legendary Lorna

Oare, Somerset

Visit the little church at the Exmoor village of Oare and you plunge straight into the story of the lovely Lorna Doone, said to have been married here and to have been shot by a jealous suitor, the brutal robber Carver Doone.

So powerful is the story of the Doones, of Lorna and her true love, the decent yeoman John Ridd, that in a remarkable piece of eccentric inversion, romance has overpowered reality and turned the story of Lorna Doone into a matter of fact rather than fiction. Even today, there are those who will tell you, with some certainty, that the Doones lived in Exmoor's remote and beautiful Lank Combe, itself now known as the Doone Valley. Exmoor has certainly profited from the story; and why not? Its beautiful landscape is the real star of the Lorna Doone story.

There is some evidence that, during the 17th century, an outlaw tribe did live within the depths of Exmoor and that they may have been the remnants of a disaffected Scottish family that had been cheated of its land in Scotland. Outlawed by King James I, the story goes, members of this family wandered into the remote fastness of Exmoor, where they and their descendants became successful and violent robbers who terrorized the neighbourhood.

It was this already romantic tale that the Victorian novelist Richard

LEFT: ***Of all the river banks in all the world...' John Ridd meets Lorna Doone for the first time in the wilds of Exmoor and a 'reality' myth is born.***

PREVIOUS PAGE: ***The Pantheon at Stourhead exemplifies the perfect merging of garden folly with the classical ideals of architecture.***

Doddridge Blackmore took as the basis of one of the most successful novels of the 19th century. Blackmore's family had lived in the area from late medieval times and his grandfather was the rector of Oare in the 1830s during Blackmore's boyhood. *Lorna Doone* was published in 1869 and became one of the most widely read novels of the 19th century. Its attraction is such that tens of thousands of visitors still visit Exmoor today, in part hooked on the romantic and powerful image of the beautiful heiress kidnapped by the robber Doones, and yet redeemed through love and courage.

There Be Big Cats Out There

Exmoor, Somerset

Once upon a time, people were convinced that there were dragons in the heathen hills and woods. Now, it seems, we are still fascinated by the possibility that the British countryside harbours exotic beasts or 'big cats' such as pumas, panthers, leopards and lynxes.

Believers say that big cats have either escaped from private zoos unreported, or were released by irresponsible owners, when the Dangerous Wild Animals Act of 1976 made the (expensive) licensing of such creatures compulsory. Dead livestock found with unexplained and often savage wounds have fuelled the myth of the big cat. Each year, several hundred sightings of mysterious creatures are reported from all parts of the country, although south-west England remains the most fruitful beast-spotting area of all, with people now producing video-footage of distant blobs, moving cat-like along field edges. The far west of Cornwall has its Morvah Puma, mid Cornwall has its Beast of Bodmin Moor, and many other parts of Devon and Somerset have produced reports of big cat sightings. Exmoor has been a fruitful big cat ground for many years and has seen some intensive investigation, including deployment of Royal Marine spotters and sharpshooters.

In the mid 1990s, British Government scientists investigated claims of big cat sightings and concluded that there was no verifiable evidence of exotic species running wild anywhere in Britain. Investigators stated that wound marks on dead farm animals could have been caused by scavenging foxes or dogs, but added

ABOVE: *Behind every tree, behind every blade of grass – behind this page even – lurks a big beast...*

ABOVE: ***Andrew Crosse, a scientist who predicted that electricity would enable people 'to communicate...thoughts instantaneously with the uttermost parts of the earth.'***

that they could not state unreservedly that there were no 'escaped' big cats out there.

Discovery of a complete carcass of a puma or panther might be the clincher, but so far only skulls have turned up on Bodmin Moor, Dartmoor and Exmoor. The Bodmin Moor and Dartmoor skulls were found to be parts of tiger or leopard skin rugs, while the Exmoor skull was said to be from a stuffed panther. Undaunted, big cat spotters continue to come forward with what they believe is photographic and video evidence, while even hard-headed sceptics have been converted after claiming to have seen a big cat momentarily frozen in their car headlights or casually crossing a footpath. Eyewitness accounts, fuzzy photographs and video footage may often be discounted as sightings of foxes, dogs, domestic and feral cats – and wishful thinking. Keep your eyes peeled, all the same...

The Thunder & Lightning Man

Quantock Hills, Somerset

Mary Shelley's famous novel *Frankenstein* may have been inspired by a Victorian scientist who harnessed the power of lightning bolts for experiments in the rooms of his remote Somerset mansion.

The remarkable 19th-century scientist, Andrew Crosse, lived at Fyne Court in Somerset's peaceful Quantock Hills, where he devoted his life to investigating the theory of electricity. Crosse was a brilliant experimental scientist, but there is no doubt that he also possessed a fabulous streak of eccentricity. His spectacular, and often noisy, experiments involved rigging lightning conductors in trees and on poles in the garden of Fyne Court and wiring everything to apparatus inside the house. On really good nights an electrical charge of 100,000 volts could be channelled to measuring apparatus in Fyne Court's organ gallery. The windows of the house flared with brilliant light and loud bangs reverberated across the land. Such activity earned Crosse the sobriquet of the Thunder and Lightning Man, and more sinister accusations of wizardry.

In the 1830s, Crosse's attempts to form silicate crystals, using electricity, created what appeared to be tiny insects, though later theory suggests that the wriggling 'mites' were in fact crystals. Crosse made no claims that he had 'created' life, but others claimed it for him. It was enough to horrify the religious-bound Victorian world and Crosse was condemned by newspapers as a 'reviler of our Holy Religion'. Mary Shelley is believed to have attended a lecture given by Andrew Crosse in London and her knowledge of the controversy over Crosse's moving mites is said to have in part inspired her to write *Frankenstein.*

Crosse died in 1855 and, ironically, most of Fyne Court was destroyed by fire in 1894. The present estate and surviving buildings are now in the hands of the National Trust and are part of a nature reserve and information centre that can be visited.

Fascinating Follies of Barwick Park

Yeovil, Somerset

Just outside the town of Yeovil, on the road to Dorchester, stands a quartet of entirely useless, but fascinating, ornamental follies that mark out their originator as a creative eccentric of the highest order.

The follies of Barwick Park were paid for by the estate's 19th-century owner, the philanthropic businessman George Messiter, as a device for giving employment to redundant Yeovil glove-makers. This was an early job-creation scheme of some originality.

On the north side of the park is the Fish Tower, a 15-metre (50-foot) column on a square base, with a door to its interior; a weathervane, in the form of a fish, once stood on the top. To the west is a very tall pointed cone peppered with square slots and standing on a base that is pierced by open arches. To the south is a true obelisk, with a crooked top, and Jack The Treacle Eater, an arch of rubblestone supporting a short tower and steeple crowned by the elegant figure of the ancient Greek messenger god, Hermes. It represents a servant of the Messiters who lived in the tower and whose duties included carrying messages on foot to and from London. He was said to eat treacle as part of his training regime and you may still be told that if a basin of treacle is left by the tower at night, it's licked clean in the morning. Foxes are fast on their feet...

Tor Tales

Glastonbury, Somerset

At glorious Glastonbury, Christian symbolism and Arthurian legend jostle each other for attention, while one of the world's greatest pop music festivals echoes, in a very loud fashion, the celebratory gatherings of prehistory. There's enough eccentricity and exhibitionism in the air here to fill a fleet of hot air balloons. As it is, you may well find coloured bubbles wafting from the delightful doorways of Glastonbury's numerous 'alternative' shops.

In truth, the famous Glastonbury Music Festival takes place at Pilton, several miles from Glastonbury itself, something the good citizens of the town are quick to point out, though Glastonbury has enough wonderful attractions of its own, among which is the famous Glastonbury Tor, a smooth green hill that rises to a height of 158 metres (518 feet) above the town. On top stands the ruined tower of St Michael's Church. At the foot of the Tor is the Chalice Well, also known as the Blood Spring, said

BELOW: ***Jack the Treacle Eater's Tower at Barwick Park. Jack was a messenger who ran regularly between Yeovil and London, sticking to his routine by training on treacle.***

to have healing qualities associated with the legend of the Holy Grail.

Glastonbury's Christian-Arthurian associations run deep. Legend says that Joseph of Arimathea visited the area and hid the Holy Grail containing Christ's blood in the well, thus causing the waters to turn blood red in colour. A high iron content in the local ground soil may explain both the red discolouration of the water and its health-giving qualities, but who dares spoil a good story?

BELOW: ***The tower of St Michael's Church atop Glastonbury Tor; a magnet for dreams and destinations.***

In the town itself the splendid ruins of the 10th-century Glastonbury Abbey continue the Christian-Arthurian connection. The abbey began as a simple chapel in the 2nd century AD, built by missionaries sent from Rome. It is this verifiable fact that has given rise to claims that Joseph of Arimathea, armed with the Holy Grail and various other sainted relics, was among these earliest Christian settlers.

The abbey also has a claim to be the burial place of King Arthur and his Queen, Guinevere. In the 12th century, the abbey monks discovered bones in a grand grave in the grounds and quickly let it be known that these were the bones of the royal pair. It must have been the earliest example of quick-thinking tourism promotion; pilgrims thronged to the abbey on the strength of it all, thus rescuing the monks from threatened bankruptcy.

A Clock to Watch

Wells, Somerset

The breathtaking Wells Cathedral can hardly be described as an 'eccentric' building. This is a deeply serious pile, the first purely Gothic cathedral in England; but hidden among the cathedral's many wonderful artefacts are some happily odd elements.

Wells Cathedral took a long time to build. Work began in 1180 but was not completed until 1340. The cathedral's west front is a major feature and inspired many of Europe's later cathedral façades. Its interior is just as awesome: the central crossing tower is 50 metres (518 feet) high and is supported by strainer arches of massive proportions resembling huge stone 'scissors' that spring directly from ground level and are met at their apex by a matching inverted arch. Add to all this splendour the cathedral's beautiful Chapter House and its numerous monuments, and the overall impression is truly awe-inspiring.

There's light relief, however. As with many medieval buildings of huge presence and dignity, stonemasons left little eccentric motifs all over the place, as if to reassert a sense of everyday humanity. Look closely at the decorative stone foliage of the interior piers that support the cathedral's roof and you may spot a tiny farmer chasing a fox, a man plucking a thorn from his foot, another having his tooth taken out and mischievous boys stealing fruit. On the outer walls are statues and gargoyles, including representations of modern masons who were involved in restoration work. One smiling face is complete with stone spectacles.

But the cathedral's oddest and most fascinating feature is its famous clock, one of the oldest in the world, and dated to 1392, although the original works are now in the London Science Museum. The clock is in the north transept and you'll have to join the crowds eager to view the flurry of activity as the clock's mechanisms whirr into life on every quarter and a little figure, known as Jack Blandifer, wallops the bells while jousting knights chase each other around the base. On the outside wall of the transept is a simpler but elegant clock face, with two quarter-jacks in 15th-century armour.

Getting Nettled

Marshwood, Dorset

The longest sting in the world takes place each year at the Dorset village of Marshwood, when the World Nettle-eating Championship brings together a host of competitors, eager to get their teeth nettled. The rules are simple. The winner is the person who eats the most nettles, although the clincher is the collective length of nettles swallowed.

The nettle – or, to give it its posh name, *Urtica dioica* – has long been a dietary delight, but only when rendered into soup, a concoction of Urtica with other vegetables, rice, cream and stock, the entire mass puréed into something quite exquisite and tender to the taste.

Like many great eccentricities, competitive nettle-eating started out in a pub. Some time in the 1980s, that long desultory decade, two Dorset farmers were enjoying a pint in Marshwood's popular Bottle Inn and fell to arguing about the amount of nettles that annually infested their land. Both became nettled over the other's claim to have the longest nettles ever and the landlady artfully took the sting out of the debate by suggesting that a Longest Nettle Championship should be staged during Marshwood's annual Midsummer Madness Festival. Again in the best traditions of great British eccentricity, one competitor entered a specimen that measured just under 40 centimetres (15 feet 6 inches) and, in a burst of nettlish pride, stated that if anyone produced a longer nettle, he'd eat it. A visiting American couple promptly produced a longer one and the chastened challenger gamely tucked in. Nettle-eating, as a sport, was born.

Now the battle of the nettle-noshers is on at every Midsummer Madness Festival in Marshwood, where recent champions have polished off over 21 metres (69 feet) of the stinging stuff.

ABOVE: *The Bells! The Bells! at Wells... Outside version of Wells Cathedral's famous clock.*

A Giant Streaker

Cerne Abbas, Dorset

The Giant of Cerne Abbas would be arrested if he got up and walked. But this huge figure, outlined in chalk on a Dorset hillside in all his rampant nakedness, erect phallus and all, remains trapped *in solo flagrante.*

The giant lies on the west-facing slope of Giant's Hill, above the charming and emphatically modest village of Cerne Abbas. The outline of the figure is formed by a chalk-filled trench about half a metre wide. The figure is 55 metres (180 feet) tall and brandishes a club that is 37 metres (120 feet) long.

'My father added to the size of his family with the birth of my half-sister Silvy – whose conception had been assisted by fertility rites performed on the Cerne Abbas Giant.'

Marquess of Bath

Featured also are nipples, ribs, the monumental phallus – all 7 metres (23 feet) of it – eyebrows, eyes and mouth. You can view him, at an angle, from a parking place at the foot of Giant's Hill; surely the only example of officially organized voyeurism in Britain.

Legend claims the giant as a pagan icon, yet there are no recorded references to him before the 18th century, although a pagan god was certainly worshipped in the area in pre-Christian times and the present giant may have been created by lusty locals nurturing fond folk memories. During the 18th century there was a fashion for carving the shapes of horses and giant figures across the grassy slopes of England's chalk hills.

Locals seemed enthusiastic about His Mightiness, as he was known. Maypole dances took place inside a small enclosure called The Trendle that stands on the slope above the giant's head, and a marriage was sure to prove fruitful if consummated on the tip of the phallus.

Polite Victorian society was horrified by all of this. The giant's high point was often covered with bracken and an old print of Cerne Abbas shows a rather crestfallen giant in the background wearing a ludicrous nappy.

Today the giant is in the care of the National Trust and is carefully manicured each year. Direct access to the figure is not permitted, lest erosion wear him down. He is, in truth, a magnificent and eccentric rejection of prudishness. The line from Shelley's poem *Ozymandias* springs usefully to mind: 'Look on my works ye mighty, and despair...'

We do indeed.

BELOW: ***'Look on my works ye mighty, and despair...' The Cerne Abbas Giant, on Giant's Hill, makes no bones about his bounty.***

Great Globe Gazing

Swanage, Dorset

At Durlston Head, on the outskirts of Swanage, stands the famous Great Globe, a huge sphere of Portland stone representing the Earth; it is three metres in diameter (10 feet) and weighs over 40 tonnes (44 tons). All it lacks are the broad shoulders of a Cerne Abbas Giant to hold it aloft.

The globe is criss-crossed with lines of latitude and longitude and it bears the names of continents and major features, such as the Atlantic Ocean. The stone lies within a little amphitheatre of slabs, which themselves are inscribed with geographical facts, intriguing statistics, quotations from classical writers and Biblical tracts.

This last offers a clue as to how these strange testaments originated. They were the inspiration of a pious and wealthy Victorian businessman and philanthropist, George Burt, who owned a number of local quarries in the area. Burt had a social conscience, religious convictions, vast wealth, and the classical eccentricity that often went with being a successful entrepreneur in the 19th century. His determination to improve the lot of his fellows led him to create a public park at Durlston Head for the people of Swanage to enjoy free of charge. Recreation for its own sake made Victorian moralists uneasy, however, and Burt installed the famous globe and other 'tablets of stone' in the hope that people would be educated while inhaling the robust fresh air of the cliff-tops.

Today the Durlston Country Park covers about 260 acres (105 hectares), where Burt's stone tracts and homilies still entertain with their Old Testament flavour.

Gap Year Gardener

Stourhead, Wiltshire

In 1740 the young Henry Hoare, scion of a wealthy banking family, returned from his Grand Tour of mainland Europe – the 18th-century version of the modern young person's 'gap year'– with eccentric, but spectacular, ideas about landscape gardening.

Henry Hoare the Elder had built the family home of Stourhead House in the Palladian style during the 1720s, and young Henry continued the theme of classical antiquity when he set to work on the garden in 1740. This fitted the fashion of the time, of creating a landscape like a two-dimensional painting in order to complement classical architecture.

Henry Junior had come home from his tour with the idea of 'educating nature, forming landscapes into compositions much as painters would do'. He succeeded in creating one of the most beautiful gardens in England.

The centrepiece of Arcadian Stourhead is the artificial lake, constructed in 1744. A journey around its banks is an allegory of Aeneas's voyage after the fall of Troy. The landscape is dotted with mock temples and other follies, including a replica of the Pantheon and the Temple of Apollo. Offstage is the delectable Doric Temple of Flora and high above, amidst deep woodland, is the circular Temple of the Sun. Throw in medieval crosses and Iron Age hill forts and Stourhead rates as one of the finest of England's great estates. Now

BELOW: *A giant gobstopper of a globe at Durlston Head gives visitors the chance for a bit of mental globetrotting.*

in the care of the National Trust, Henry Hoare's glorious garden and its house can be visited.

Holiday snaps would never have been enough for Henry.

Maud Against The Mud

Wick Hill, Wiltshire

There was a time when everyone trudging across the low-lying Wiltshire countryside in winter ended up with muddy feet. Until, that is, a 15th-century widow called Maud Heath decided to build a causeway, a stone pathway raised above ground level.

Each day, Maud would carry eggs to market, a four-mile journey on foot from her home at Wick Hill to the town of Chippenham. The route crossed the River Avon, where the land adjoining the river was often flooded. This was in pre-welly boot and waterproofing days and the Widow Heath ended up too often with soggy socks. Tired of it all, she sold some property she owned in Chippenham to pay for the building of a causeway.

Common sense suggests that a woman capable of finding enough money for the building of four miles of causeway, probably never needed to carry baskets of eggs to market for a living; but Maud Heath may well illustrate the recurring theme of eccentric wealth that sees no contradiction in spending money on a whim.

Much of the causeway is a simple raised path, but at Kellaways, where the route crosses the river, there is a proper brick-built causeway, raised above the modern road, with 64 little arches. Here there is a sundial, built a century after the causeway, with the story of Maud Heath recorded on a plaque.

Hot Bath

Longleat, Wiltshire

Eccentricity is often seen as being the prerogative of the titled and the wealthy; but you can never really buy eccentricity, and the hugely personable Alexander Thynne, 7th Marquess of Bath, stands out as an absolute authentic, if egocentric, eccentric.

Behind the bearded Bath, of course, stands ownership of the bankable Longleat Safari Park, the first place in the world, outside Africa, to establish a safari park. That Alexander Thynne can afford to indulge himself is patent. Longleat is an extremely hard-headed business venture that includes a holiday village as well as the famous wildlife park, whose equally hirsute Lions of Longleat inspired the Marquess's media nickname, the Loins of Longleat. (No slip of the pen here; the wordplay with loins arises from Lord Bath's devotion to the old hippie belief in free love and to the dizzying number – said to be over 50 – of Bathian 'wifelets' who have shared that enthusiasm with him).

The Marquess is also an enthusiastic artist, novelist and poet and has written a highly entertaining autobiography, *Strictly Private*, in which he tells of his colourful life, starting with his days at prep school and Eton College. Lord Bath is famed for the exuberant and colourful murals ('pornographic pizzas', as one commentator memorably called them) with which he has covered the walls of Longleat House itself, which can be visited as well as the Safari Park.

There have been other titled oddballs, but often dismayed ones, trapped in a downward spiral of drink and drug abuse, their eccentricities being too often negative and brutally destructive of ultimately grey lives. The Marquess of Bath is full Technicolor and is life-affirming.

On the top of Wick Hill is a statue of Widow Heath perched rather sternly on top of a pillar, complete with shawl and basket of eggs, a fond reminder of her daily walk to market and her legacy, long appreciated by local people and still appreciated today by increasing numbers of recreational walkers.

A Massive Molehill

Silbury Hill, Wiltshire

Ancient Britons certainly liked to make a mountain out of a molehill, if the spectacular prehistoric mini-peak of Silbury Hill is anything to go by.

Silbury Hill is the largest man-made mound in Europe. It rises from the grassy Wiltshire countryside, south of the great stone ring at Avebury, and alongside the A4 Marlborough to Chippenham road. The hill is nearly 40 metres (131 feet) tall; it covers an area of around 2 hectares (5½ acres) and contains 12.5 million cubic feet of soil. The tools used to build it would have been made of antler, bone and wood and it is estimated that it must have taken 500 workers ten years to build. Archaeologists have dated the hill to about 2100 BC, the transitional period between Stone Age and Bronze Age; a time before most of the great standing stones at nearby Avebury were erected.

There have been many excavations and explorations of Silbury over the centuries. In 1776, the Duke of Northumberland paid Cornish miners to sink a shaft from the top of the hill, but no hidden chamber graves or artefacts were found. Modern investigations have revealed that the hill was built in several stages. It began as a mere pimple, 5 metres (16 feet) high, then rose to 17 metres (56 feet), and then to its present height. It was found that the hill was reinforced with interior walls of chalk to ensure that water drained away and that the weight of the hill did not collapse upon itself.

It is known that Silbury was used by the Romans as a survey point and that the Saxons turned it into a fort, but its original purpose remains shrouded in mystery. It may have been constructed simply as a hill amid a land of fairly unrelenting flatness; a ceremonial focal point for the surrounding population. What is certain is that Silbury Hill represents a remarkable feat of engineering. It was meant to last and has survived for over 4000 years – just a little bit longer than many modern 'wonders' of architecture.

OPPOSITE: *Widow Heath keeping her feet dry atop her memorial column on Wick Hill.*

BELOW: *Silbury Hill near Avebury in Wiltshire can show us a thing or two about genuine 'millennium domes'.*

Surrey, Oxfordshire & Berkshire

Home Counties is the rather homely term attached to the counties that encircle London and that are being increasingly engulfed by the great city. Surrey and Berkshire fit neatly inside the ring, with Oxfordshire not far beyond. All have sacrificed some of their identities to the capital's voracious spread, but are still rich in history and have been the stage for great events that are echoed today in sumptuous royal ceremonies at Windsor Castle and in great traditional institutions such as Oxford University. Here, too, the old and the new, the stately and the bizarre, produce a fascinating mix that celebrates England's resilient diversity. Ancient stones still stir superstition, the surreal figure of a horse, cherished for 2000 years, is tattooed onto a green hillside, ferocious gargoyles enliven the medieval façades of stately buildings – and a huge shark's tail protrudes from the roof of a suburban semi.

Garters, Gargoyles & Great White Sharks

An Upside-down View of Things

Coldharbour, Surrey

Wealthy 18th-century eccentric Richard Hull enjoyed being head and shoulders above the crowd, but left instructions to reverse the order of things on his death. He was buried head downwards.

In 1766, Hull built himself a handsome Prospect Tower on top of his property of Leith Hill at Coldharbour, south of Dorking. The top of the tower is 313 metres (1027 feet) above sea level and is the highest point in south-east England. The views are spectacular. On a clear day you can see London's modest skyscrapers, the busy shipping lanes of the English Channel, the South Downs, the North Downs, the Chilterns, the Kent Hills and even Gatwick Airport.

By the early 19th century, Prospect Tower had begun to crumble, but was rescued and renovated in 1864. Vandals had filled the interior with rubble and cement and a new flight of steps had to be built on the outside. The tower is now owned by the National Trust and is open to the public, but you need to walk for a steepish half-mile from the car park to get there. It's worth it.

LEFT: *Beneath Leith Hill Tower lies Richard Hull, buried upside down because he believed that the world will turn topsy turvy on Judgement Day.*

PREVIOUS PAGE: *Deep dive diverted. The magnificent Headington Shark tails off through the roof of a suburban semi in Oxford.*

Richard Hull carried eccentricity to the grave. He believed that on Judgement Day the world would be turned upside down. When he died in 1772, in keeping with his instructions, he was buried head downward beneath the tower, so that on the Last Day he would meet his Maker as upstandingly as he had lived.

Today, there's a café in the base of the tower, and visitors sip tea and nibble cakes over Richard Hull's up-ended bones.

Mary's Marvellous Mortuary

Compton, Surrey

The Victorian artist Mary Watts did not let death dull her vision. She created a heavenly mortuary chapel, just for the hell of it.

Mary was married to the distinguished 19th-century painter and sculptor George Frederick Watts, best known for his allegorical paintings of great historical themes and for his monumental sculptures of such equally monumental subjects as the poet Alfred, Lord Tennyson. The couple lived at Compton, near Guildford. Mary was herself an accomplished painter. She had an enduring love of the motifs and symbols of so-called Celtic art, the ancient imagery of Iron Age Britain and Ireland.

When the churchyard at Compton filled up with too many tenants, a new burial ground was planned and Mary Watts decided that it should have its own chapel. She had no architectural skills, but, nothing daunted, she set out to design and build the chapel of her dreams. Mary taught clay-modelling to local people and recruited her students to make bricks, with which the mortuary chapel, an attractive Italianate building, was erected. It was tiled with terracotta, and strikes a suitably sober graveyard note. But Mary Watts's eccentric vision transformed the vaulted interior into a cornucopia of exquisite murals and reliefs featuring saints and angels and much gold interlacing.

The chapel took four years to build and was completed in 1898. Today it is surrounded by tall Irish yew trees that were planted by Mary Watts, who lies at peace, and no doubt with great satisfaction, in the cemetery.

RIGHT: ***Mary Watts knew what was what when it came to sublime design. Her mortuary chapel at Compton is a glorious celebration of unique art work.***

ABOVE: *Lingfield Lockup is something of a modern* des. res. *when it comes to location.*

LOCKUP LOCATION, LOCATION, LOCATION

Lingfield, Surrey

The oft-quoted line 'Stone walls do not a prison make' may be one of the most desperate pieces of wishful thinking around, but when it comes to location, location, location, the old village 'lockups' of England almost measure up to desirable residence status.

One of the quaintest of these little local prisons is The Cage in the Surrey village of Lingfield. The Lingfield lockup stands by the village pond in the shade of a huge oak tree that is said to be over 400 years old. It is part of a grouping that includes the medieval St Peter's Cross, an old boundary marker that delineated two properties.

The Cage dates from 1773 and was used for securing local villains and drunks, often prior to their being carted off to court. There were similar lockups all over England; some contained stocks, just to make sure. Many reflected the mores of a fiercely judgmental society. The lockup at Swanage in Dorset, for example, bore the inscription: 'Erected for the prevention of vice and immorality by the friends of religion and good order'; enough to send a shiver of guilt down anyone's spine.

Lingfield's little lockup was last used in 1882 when a local poacher was incarcerated there. It seems obvious that the village must have acquired a new clink soon after, since even the fine upstanding citizens of this lovely part of Surrey could hardly have become entirely law-abiding overnight. Most lockups became redundant around this time as larger gaols were built.

The lockup at Lingfield has been back in service in recent times for the admirable purpose of raising cash for charities. Brave volunteers are happy to be locked up for as long as 48 hours, or until a certain amount of cash is raised for good causes. Hostages to fortune, to say the least.

THE HIGH HORSE OF UFFINGTON

Uffington Hill, Oxfordshire

The White Horse of Uffington is a dynamic, abstract representation of a huge galloping horse cut into the underlying chalk of the grassy Uffington Hill – for all the world like some racy sportswear logo. Yet this is ancient symbolism writ large, the White Horse has ridden the Downs from the time of the Iron Age at least.

Uffington's White Horse is 113 metres (372 feet) long and 40 metres (130 feet) deep and its influence has been so compelling that the great flat valley below the Downs has been known as the Vale of the White Horse for centuries.

First recorded over 900 years ago, the horse was previously thought to date from the 9th century AD, perhaps carved to celebrate the victory of King Alfred over the Danes. But modern research suggests that it is much older and that the late Iron Age, the so-called Celtic era, has prior claim. Iron Age chieftains certainly adored their horses. They were said to bathe with them and to engage in equine rituals that verged on the obscene. In the hills below the White Horse is a natural amphitheatre called The Manger that might easily have served as a ready-made corral for Iron Age horses. And just over the brow of the hill is Uffington Castle, an extensive hill settlement of the Iron Age.

Some people have claimed that the horse represents a dragon, or a cat even, but the White Horse simply kicks its heels with contempt. From the medieval period onwards local people scoured the outline of the horse every seven years to keep it fresh. The scouring was accompanied by a riotous festival of horse-racing, cheese-rolling, wrestling, dancing and feasting.

Today, the White Horse is carefully protected by the National Trust. Uffington Hill is open to visitors, although the angle at which the White Horse lies means that it is almost impossible to get a clear view of it from the ground, an anomaly that has given rise to more than one suggestion that the true significance of this strange carving lies somewhere out of this world.

ABOVE: ***Stoke Row's water well brings a magical maharajah makeover to deepest Oxfordshire.***

THE WELL-WISHER OF VARANASI

Stoke Row, Oxfordshire

At the village of Stoke Row in the heart of the very English Chiltern Hills lies a little bit of India, an elaborate water well, the gift of a benevolent maharajah.

During the 1850s, the maharajah was ruler of Benares, the modern Varanasi, on the banks of the River Ganges, where water was never in short supply. One day, the then Governor of the North-West Provinces, Edward Reade, was dining with the maharajah and happened to mention that in his home area of the Chilterns water was always in short supply. He spoke of Stoke in particular, mentioning how villagers rarely had clean clothes, the nearest spring being several miles away.

In a burst of characteristic generosity the maharaja offered to solve the problem by building a well in the village. Of course, being a gift from a prince, it was no ordinary well: it was 34 metres (112 feet) deep, was crowned by a gilded dome and its wellhead winding gear was topped off with a cast-iron elephant. The well cost the enormous sum, for the time, of £353. The maharajah gave further money to build a well-keeper's cottage and to plant a cherry orchard.

'THE GREAT POINT OF THE TOWER IS THAT IT WILL BE ENTIRELY USELESS...'

Lord Berners view of Faringdon Folly

The Maharajah's Well could produce hundreds of gallons a day and provided the village's water supply for 70 years, until piped water was installed. The well was renovated in the 1950s and still stands today, a token of a remarkable gesture. Local people have returned the favour – by raising money to build wells in dusty Indian villages.

THE FOLLY WITH A SPLIT PERSONALITY

Faringdon Hill, Oxfordshire

High on the wooded Faringdon Hill, between Oxford and Swindon, stands what is claimed to be the last great folly to be built in England, although it may be folly to make such a claim.

Faringdon Folly dates from 1935 and was the inspiration of the 14th Baron Berners, a man who was not going to let the changing times of the 20th century limit his view. When Lord Berners announced plans for his folly, there was ferocious opposition. The local council had been told that Berners planned to build a lighthouse on top of Faringdon Hill, complete with revolving beam of light and stentorian fog horn. The fact that Faringdon was a good 100 kilometres from the sea clearly rang a lot of bells, not to mention fog horns, in the minds of the council's planning committee. They refused permission for the tower.

Berners won the day eventually, however, and his folly arose on Faringdon Hill, though not without further eccentric dealings. He gave the job of designing the tower to his friend Lord Gerald Wellesley and then went off to Rome for a holiday. Berners returned, fired with images of Gothic grandeur on top of Faringdon Hill, but instead found a plain, uninspiring building taking shape. It was too late to start again, but Berners insisted that the tower should be finished to his design; thus, the bottom of

LEFT: ***Faringdon Folly is said to be the last great 'traditional' folly to be built in England. It neatly fits the bill of being 'entirely useless', according to Baron Berners, who commissioned it in the 1930s.***

the 30-metre (98-foot) tower is a dull square, while the top is a handsome octagon, complete with battlements.

The decaying tower was restored in 1986 and is open for visits on the first Sunday of every month, from Easter until October. From the top you can gaze out, in clear weather, across five counties. Lord Berners had the last eccentric word, as always. At the top of the tower he placed a notice, warning that anyone committing suicide did so at their own risk.

Gargling Grotesques

Oxford, Oxfordshire

The university city of Oxford may have dreaming spires, but its exquisite buildings also nurture some nightmarish features amid their stony foliage. These are the famous Oxford gargoyles and grotesques, those marvellous accents on medieval churches and buildings that serve as eccentric relief amid more formal architecture.

Think gargoyle and the word 'gargle' grabs you by the throat. Both words derive from *gargouille*, an old French word for 'throat', which in turn derives from the Latin *gurgulio*. The sound of gurgling runs through it all, and gurgle is exactly what the original gargoyles did. They were incorporated into roof gullies as spouts in order to throw rainwater clear of the walls and foundations of buildings, thus protecting the stonework from dampness and erosion. It was not until lead drainpipes were introduced in the 16th century that the gargoyle became an ornament in its own right.

Gargoyles were entirely functional, but their design motifs were wholly eccentric, especially in the context of a sacred building. Most were carved into fantastic and fiendish forms: distorted devils' heads with gaping mouths; fantastical monsters harnessed to the service of the Church. It was hardly surprising that they soon acquired a reputation for scaring off evil spirits in their turn. In time, the word 'gargoyle' came to embrace other carved creatures, known as grotesques, that had always been added to buildings simply as decorative features.

Some of the finest gargoyles and grotesques can be seen on the walls of Oxford buildings. The Church of St Mary the Virgin on High Street has a marvellous clutch of winged beasts and hooded figures, most of them best viewed from the church tower, with even finer views of Oxford beyond. In the quadrangle of Magdalen College you'll find a superb collection of medieval grotesques, known as the Hieroglyphicals, because there is no explanation of their remarkably surreal quality or what they represented.

ABOVE AND BELOW: *Getting to grips with gargoyles and grotesques in Oxford.*

Shark Attic!

Headington, Oxfordshire

Just when you thought it was safe to go out on the streets of the Oxford suburb of Headington, there's a shark attack – or attic, rather.

On New High Street in Headington, there stands a terrace of unassuming houses, all of them unchallenging in architecture, unassuming in façade, unsensational overall – apart from the one with the 8-metre (26-foot) Great White Shark sticking out of its roof. The shark's head is buried in the roof slates, its elegant tail pointing at the sky, as if it has just plunged from the heavens in one great tail-slapping leap from the southern oceans – or during a particularly heavy rainstorm.

This spectacular piece of roofscape is in fact a work of art known as *Untitled, 1986*. Created by sculptor John Buckley, the huge fibreglass shark was installed on 9th August, 1986, the 41st anniversary of the dropping of the first nuclear bomb on the Japanese city of Nagasaki. The 'installation' was said to be a gesture against nuclear fission and such nuclear horrors as Nagasaki and Chernobyl. How the shark symbolism fitted the bill is uncertain, but whatever the details, the Headington Shark was a magnificently creative and eccentric gesture of epic proportions.

As soon as the shark appeared, neighbours and the local council objected. The council ordered immediate removal of the great beast, on the grounds that it was a danger to the public. But the shark was as much a brilliant piece of engineering as an art installation. It was supported by reinforced roof girders and experts declared it safe. The council then decided that the shark was in breach of planning regulations.

The War of the Headington Shark went on for several years, until, in 1992, a government planning inspector made a decision allowing *Untitled, 1986* to remain in situ. His ruling is one of the most uplifting decisions ever made in the name of dull bureaucracy, and reads: 'Any system of control must make some small place for the dynamic, the unexpected, the downright quirky. I therefore recommend that the Headington

BELOW: ***Failed quiz-show contestants, gnarly knights, or a load of old rollrocks at Long Compton?***

Shark be allowed to remain.' And so, in a magnificent triumph of originality over the ordinary, the Great White remains as the world's ultimate shark attic.

A Right Royal Rollright

Little Rollright, Oxfordshire

The dramatic Rollright Stones stand on a chalk ridge above the villages of Long Compton and Little Rollright on the Oxfordshire-Warwickshire border. Like other stone clusters, they were probably once part of an ancient burial chamber or ceremonial site, although legend won't settle for that. For centuries, local people gathered at Rollright to press their ears against the rough limestone pillars, known as the Whispering Knights, and listen to them murmur secrets and prophecies. People would cut the trunk of a nearby elder tree and, as the sap oozed out, it was said that the largest stone of all, the King Stone, 'turned its head'. At midnight, the stones are said to roll right down the hill to drink at a spring near little Rollright. All perfectly normal behaviour for the Home Counties.

The popular legend behind the Rollright Stones tells of an ancient chieftain who was hell-bent on the conquest of all England. He and his followers were striding along above Long Compton when they decided to take a tea break. The man who would be king, pondering the coming battles, wandered off alone. He bumped into a local witch, whose job was, essentially, a game show hostess of antiquity full of teasing questions and dangerous challenges. The witch told the chieftain that he might well become king of all England if, within seven strides, he could see the village of Long Compton below.

Confident of the broad prospect from the ridge, the chieftain strode forth with some arrogance, only to find his view blocked by an ancient burial mound. His forfeit was suitably Draconian and, with a triumphant cackle worthy of Anne Robinson, the witch turned the would-be king and his cronies to stone. Just like that.

The witch was so excited that she seems to have turned herself into an elder tree by mistake. Would that all game show hosts and hostesses...

Glorious Garter

Windsor, Berkshire

On the 19th June each year, several of Britain's high-ranking nobles gather at the royal residence of Windsor Castle – and put on garters.

Boldly said, this sounds like the final irrefutable evidence of an irreversibly batty Britain; but Windsor's Knights of the Garter Ceremony represents British tradition at its most profound, and royal ceremony at its most dignified.

The Order of the Knights of the Garter is extremely select. There are never more than 24 Knights Companion of the Order, plus The Royal Knights. The Order was created by Edward III in 1348 and is the oldest and most senior British Order of Chivalry, awarded for loyalty and for military merit.

The Garter Ceremony is one of the most colourful of all Britain's Heritage events. Bands of the Royal Household Division are in full flow and squadrons of the Household Cavalry, in scarlet ceremonial uniforms, line the route taken by the Knights. All the Knights wear blue velvet robes with red hoods draped over the right shoulder. On their heads are black velvet hats with white plumes. The badge of the Order, a St George's Cross within a garter framed by silver beams, is worn on the left shoulder.

The most eccentric explanation of how the Garter originated relates to a royal ball in which Edward III was dancing with the Countess of Salisbury whose blue garter fell to the floor. Why it did so is anyone's guess; but the king retrieved it and rather dashingly tied it to his own leg. Watching courtiers sniggered, as is their wont, but were angrily silenced by the king, who allegedly made the famous comment, *'Honi soit qui mal y pense'*, Norman French being the order of the day. This translates as 'Shame on him who thinks this evil' – a perfect motto for a new Order of Chivalry soon to be introduced.

Hardheaded historians argue that the Garter derives instead from the use of armour straps and that the motto refers to more serious political matters relating to Edward's claims to the French throne. There is no record of what the countess thought, or whether or not she got her garter back.

Hampshire & Sussex

England's south coast counties of Hampshire and Sussex have long been a historic gateway to the nation. It was at Hastings, on the coast of East Sussex, that the old Britain of the Anglo Saxons and the Danes succumbed to the Norman Conquest as yet another wave of powerful and fruitful influences and values overlaid, and was absorbed by, the existing culture of the island race. Inland from the famous chalk cliffs of Beachy Head lie the South Downs, a sylvan bulwark between the great conurbation of London and such famous coastal resorts as Brighton. This is an area that thrives on the diversity of custom and tradition, where a world-famous gathering of vintage cars is matched by the crazy sport of lawnmower racing, where grown men and women leap into the sea dressed in crazy costumes, and where quirky buildings pepper the landscape.

Fabulous Follies, Batty Birdmen, Guys, Garlic & A Great Beast

Hold Your Breath

Isle of Wight, Hampshire

'Anyone for garlic ice cream?' is not entirely the kind of cry that would draw the seaside crowds, but at the Garlic Festival every August on the Isle of Wight you can even sample a garlic beer after your garlic ice cream. Whether or not garlic and chips would ever catch on is anyone's vampire. The Isle of Wight Garlic Festival grew from bulb-like beginnings in the early 1980s to a successful annual event. The island is a major producer of the pungent perennial.

Garlic originated in Asia, swept the Mediterranean and is now a fixture on the world's culinary scene. It has a hallowed reputation as a protection against vampires, especially in central Europe and the old regions of Transylvania and Bohemia, regular hangouts of battishness. Even corpses were buried there with their orifices stuffed with garlic bulbs; people smeared garlic on the foreheads of sleeping infants and hung garlic flowers over windows and doorways as protection against the bloodsuckers. Bram Stoker's famous novel *Dracula* boosted the image even more.

How the garlic-against-the-vampire tradition began is vague, but one suggestion is that medieval shepherds in Bohemia used to feed small amounts of arsenic to their flocks, and even to themselves, because vampires – either bats or the alleged human version – were repelled by the taint of arsenic in the blood. Garlic later became a healthier substitute because of an alleged similarity in odour between garlic and burning arsenic.

All this vampirism apart, garlic's true reputation rests on its culinary excellence and on its claimed health-giving qualities. The Isle of Wight festival does an outstanding job of promoting the breathy bulb and features a fantastic variety of garlicky treats, from the aforementioned ice cream, to smoked garlic, vampire relish, garlic-flavoured sausages and a range of other splendid foods. Just air kiss while you're at it...

A Three In One Servant

Minstead, Hampshire

A madly eccentric sign, featuring a very odd creature indeed, hangs outside the Trusty Servant pub in Minstead in the heart of the New Forest. Pictured on the sign is a bizarre representation of a hybrid of pig, donkey and deer;

RIGHT: ***Highclere Castle interiors embrace every possible design flourish of the 19th century.***

OPPOSITE: ***Minstead's Trusty Servant pub sign rings the changes on the ideal servant.***

PREVIOUS PAGE: ***In lieu of any practical flying potential, this Bognor Birdman definitely pulled the plug on any hope of horizontal flight.***

not the disastrous result of modern genetic engineering, but the idealized image of a 16th-century servant, carrying a variety of tools and implements, a padlock, a sword and a shield.

The original sign is thought to date from the 16th century and came from Winchester College at a time long before the days of impoverished students living in grubby bed-sits. In those days, the elite scions of wealthy families were waited on hand and foot while at college. They were troublesome young delinquents, who required a very special kind of servant.

The various features of the bizarre figure on the pub sign represent the attributes of just such a servant: the donkey for tireless patience, the deer for swiftness, the sword and shield for protecting young masters – and, perhaps less flatteringly, the pig for a willingness to eat all the food scraps. The locked padlock represents the trusty servant's ability to keep safe any scandalous secrets. The verse displayed below the sign says it all:

A Trusty Servant's portrait would you see,
This Emblematic Figure well survey.
The Porker's Snout not nice in diet shows,
The Padlock shut no secrets he'll disclose.
Patient the Ass his Master's wrath will bear
Swiftness in errand the Stagg's feet declare.
Loaded his Left Hand apt to labour saith,
The Vest his neatness, Open hand his faith.
Girt with his Sword, his Shield upon his arm,
Himself and master he'll protect from harm.

High Victorian Highclere

Highclere, Hampshire

If money buys eccentric indulgence, then Highclere Castle near Newbury represents the pinnacle of 19th-century quirkiness and exuberance.

The castle was designed in the 1830s for the 3rd Earl of Carnarvon by Charles Barry, the inspired designer of the Houses of Parliament. Highclere's grand pinnacled pile was completed in 1842.

Splendid though the exterior of Highclere is, the interior is the ultimate expression of the Carnarvons' wealth and taste. Barry and other high flying architects

ABOVE: ***Chocks away! at Bognor for a real effort that sadly ended up in the drink.***

of the day designed a series of rooms that reflect just about every grand style of the time, including Gothic fan vaulting, the exquisite designs of Moorish Spain, and rococo extravagance. The furnishings are just as eclectic. The Carnarvons were enthusiastic collectors and among Highclere's artefacts are paintings by such masters as Van Dyck, while other items include Napoleon's desk and chair, acquired from the exile's home of St Helena by the 3rd Earl in 1827.

The 5th Earl of Carnarvon inherited the family's extraordinary interests. He was a dedicated archaeologist and Egyptologist and was among those who discovered the tomb of Tutankhamun in 1922. Ever acquisitive, Carnarvon acquired from the tomb a collection of items, which lay unseen in the cellars of Highclere until their discovery in 1988, since when they have been on display in the castle.

Not content with a fascinating house, the Carnarvons created a marvellous garden to surround Highclere. Features include an exotic Orangery and Fernery as well as a Secret Garden of walled walkways. Highclere can be visited during the months of July and August.

Favoured Mount at Farley Mount

Farley Mount Country Park, Hampshire

Favoured horses are often mourned by their owners with inordinate sentimentality, but few have merited such equine adulation as the favourite of wealthy 18th-century landowner Paulet St John, who built a special mausoleum for his hunter on a hilltop in Hampshire.

The Farley Mount Horse Mausoleum lies in the attractive Farley Mount Country Park, 4 kilometres (2½ miles) west of Winchester, and has been refurbished in recent years. The original was thought to have been a fairly mundane square structure that was replaced at some time in the 19th century with the present sharply pointed pyramid, a gleaming white building that can be seen from miles around. The mausoleum has porches on its four sides; three are blank, but the fourth gives access to the interior, where a plaque tells the story of the buried horse beneath your feet.

Paulet St John was an enthusiastic fox hunter and one day, while racing at great speed across country, he and his trusty steed fell into a chalk pit that was 7.5 metres (25 feet) deep. So adept was the horse that it landed unscathed, without even unseating the Hon. Paulet, who thereafter dubbed it, with a flash of extreme originality, Beware Chalk Pit. BCP won several races thereafter and was so beloved by its master that instead of being buried in a chalk pit, earned itself the ultimate high horse accolade by being buried on a hilltop crowned by a 9-metre (30-foot) high mausoleum. For the rest of us, the views of the rolling Hampshire countryside are exhilarating.

Flights of Fancy in Bognor

Bognor Regis, Sussex

Pigs may or may not fly, but every year at the seaside town of Bognor Regis you'll get a grandstand view of flying folk, as dozens of very short-haul eccentrics throw themselves off the end of Bognor Pier, dressed in ridiculous costumes and attached to bizarre contraptions.

This is no lemming-like fancy dress parade, but the determined pursuit of a £15,000 prize awarded to

whoever can propel themselves 100 metres (328 feet) before splashdown, without recourse to any form of fuel-propelled flight. Very few make it beyond nose-dive limit; but that's half the fun.

The Bognor Birdman Competition began life in 1974 at Selsey, when the Royal Airforce Association offered a prize of £3000 to anyone who could fly, without assisted power, a distance of 45 metres (150 feet) from the lifeboat platform at Selsey Bill. Although the longest flight covered only 44 metres (145 feet), the contest caused great interest and it became an annual event. In 1978, the competition moved to Bognor and is now a national institution, at present under the wing of Richard Branson's Virgin Atlantic.

Thousands of spectators turn up each year to watch a stream of people, dressed as everything from enormous rubber ducks to space aliens, dinosaurs, and Icarian-winged oddities, leap from the end of the pier, eyes fixed on the wide blue yonder, with most of them ending up in the wide blue Bognor drink.

Besides the hilarity of the fancy-dress brigade, all of whom have no hope whatsoever of going anywhere but down, there are home-made winged contraptions, some of which make a fair bird of it. In 2003, Virgin's Richard Branson, the epitome of a genial and eccentric big boss, joined the leapers, making a peculiar sideways veer, before plummeting waterwards.

DON'T LET THE GRASS GROW UNDER YOUR WHEELS

Wisborough Green, Sussex

The thrills and spills of rally driving and the roaring excitement of a power-bike race pale into insignificance in the face of the lawnmower racers of Wisborough Green.

It all began one beer-fuelled night in 1973 in the local pub, when regulars tried to think of a cheap and accessible substitute for full-blown motor racing. Motorized bar stools were quickly dismissed, but lawnmower racing seemed a cut above the rest. A Grand Prix followed soon after.

The sport is scrupulously organized by the British Lawn Mower Racing Association (motto: *Per herbam ad astra*, 'Through grass to the stars') and is divided into three classes of racing: Group 1 is for hand-pushed mowers, and benefits natural sprinters; Group 2 is considered the most skilful as it requires the mower to have a towed seat behind it, thus demanding some formidable manoeuvring skills; Group 3 is for four-wheel, sit-on mowers. Engines are souped up, within rules, and speeds of up to 40 m.p.h. are achieved.

The contest became an annual event and received a huge boost to its prestige in 1975 when the legendary British racing driver Stirling Moss came out of retirement to enter and to win.

The World Championship takes place each year at Wisborough Green, with entrants coming from as far away as New Zealand and Hong Kong. There is also a gruelling 12-hour race that was famously completed by wild man actor Oliver Reed's lawnmower, driven at two miles an hour by Reed's gardener.

Skilled and careful though lawnmower racers are, spectacular crashes do take place. Once a runaway mower demolished the (occupied) ladies' toilet.

ABOVE: ***'Domes, arches, minarets, friezes and furbelows' at Brighton's right-on Pavilion.***

Marbles Lost and Won

Tinsley Green, Sussex

Every Good Friday, at Tinsley Green, near Crawley, large numbers of people knuckle down and get thoroughly marbled in the World Marble Championship. The championships are organized by the British Marbles Control Board and although there are endless variants of marble games, the championship involves 49 marbles being placed in a ring. The first team – of six players – to clear 25 marbles from the ring wins.

Marbles as a sport cannot avoid the flavour of eccentricity, but as a pastime it has a distinguished pedigree dating from at least Egyptian and Roman times.

Early marbles were made of clay, stone and marble itself; but it was only during the 1840s, when a German glass-blower came up with a special tool for making glass marbles, that marbles went on a roll, world-wide.

The pastime has its own patois that has given rise to a wonderful vocabulary that includes such words as marididdles, mibs, moonaggies, snooger, toe bombsie, bounce about, bounce eye, picking plums. 'Knuckling down' is a famous marble phrase that has entered the language and derives from the expert marble method of holding the marble in place above the first joint of the thumb by the tip of the forefinger. The middle finger holds the top of the thumb like a trigger and is released with whatever force is needed. It seems an awkward method, but is said to produce the greatest accuracy.

Brighton's Brightest Buildings

Brighton, Sussex

Gathering the world's most exotic architectural features into one building probably transcends eccentricity, but the magnificent Royal Pavilion at Brighton endures as a masterful merging of style with sensation. It is as satisfyingly 'off-centre' as any building could ever be.

The Pavilion is a mix of Gothic, Indian and Islamic styles that has produced an Arabian Nights fantasy. Domes, arches, minarets, friezes and furbelows all combine in this wonderful building, the high achievement of 19th century picturesque, made all the more fascinating by its proximity to the classical architecture of terraced Brighton by the sea.

The original building on the site was a modest farmhouse that had been rented by the then Prince of Wales, later to become George IV. The Prince used the cottage as a love nest for himself and his mistress, Mrs Maria Fitzherbert, whom he eventually married in a ceremony of doubtful legal validity. George later became the monstrous figure of political cartoons – 'A voluptuary under the horrors of digestion', as he was memorably captioned by the brilliant caricaturist of the day, James Gillray. But he did at least promote the conversion of his Brighton love nest into first a neo-classical villa in 1787 and then, when he became Regent in 1815, into the marvellous Pavilion that survives today, the design of the inspired architect John Nash.

The Royal Pavilion was severely damaged by a fire in the 1980s but was restored at massive expense and is open to the public.

VROOMING VETS

Brighton, Sussex

At the end of the 19th century the motor car, horseless carriage, or light locomotive, as it was variously known, was in its grizzling infancy and the world was in some turmoil over what many saw as an infernal imposition on society and a threat to life and limb. So concerned were the authorities in Britain about the potential damage that these mechanical monsters might wreak that a law was passed regulating the speed of the car to four miles per hour, with the requirement that a person had to precede the vehicle on foot, waving a red flag and glancing frequently behind.

The red flag requirement had been lifted as early as 1878, as it became obvious that the car was going to be a metaphorical runaway success. In 1896, the Locomotives on the Highway Act was passed, raising the speed limit for 'light locomotives' to 14 miles per hour. On Saturday, 14th November of that year, an Emancipation Run of vehicles was staged from London to Brighton to celebrate the passing of the new law.

This was the origin of the celebrated London to Brighton Veteran Car Run, held on the first Sunday of

BELOW: ***Tooting horns for vintage vets during the London to Brighton Veteran Car Run.***

ABOVE: *Lewes mocks the Fawkes and lights up in spectacular fashion on Bonfire Night. Effigies of George W Bush and Winnie the Pooh have even gone up in flames.*

November each year. It is not a race – few of the venerable vehicles would survive a burn-up, and their dignified nature eschews such vulgarity. Vehicles are not permitted to exceed 20 m.p.h. over the 87-kilometre (54-mile) course and the only prize is a Finisher's Medal.

The kind of top vintage car taking part is exemplified by those driven by enthusiast Prince Michael of Kent, President of the Royal Automobile Club. These include an 1899 Wolseley, a 1900 Daimler, a De Dion Bouton, a Napier racing car, a De Dietrich – all dating from 1903 – and a 1904 Mercedes. Only cars built before 1905 are eligible to take part.

The statistics are awesome: the collective value of the vehicles taking part is estimated at £40 million. Hundreds of thousands of spectators enjoy the spectacle, some lining the route, although most gather at Brighton for the marvellous sight of so many vintage cars, their drivers and passengers in vintage clothing. And not a red flag in sight.

Burning Issue

Lewes, Sussex

Guy Fawkes Night, or Bonfire Night, is one of Britain's most resilient traditions. The combination of November darkness, blazing bonfires and exploding fireworks is a sure-fire fiery draw for all ages.

Today, the tradition is being eroded because of modern strictures on safety and in response to several horrendous accidents that have turned tradition into tragedy. One place where Bonfire Night burns as bright as ever, however, is in the handsome town of Lewes, where the true political-religious roots of the tradition are celebrated with some sensation and not a little controversy.

Guy Fawkes was, of course, a would-be terrorist, one whose motives were rooted in religious dissent. On 5th November, 1605, Fawkes and a group of Roman Catholic plotters contrived to blow up the Houses of Parliament, during a full session that was attended by most of the government and by King James I, his queen and their son. The plotters hoped that, if they were successful, English Catholicism and its politics would inherit the country.

ABOVE: *Mad Jack Fuller's pyramidal mausoleum. A top-hatted Jack is said to sit patiently within upon an iron chair, ready for the Day of Reckoning.*

This was the infamous Gunpowder Plot – audacious and outrageous, but ultimately a damp squib as betrayal foiled the plot and led to the execution of the plotters and increased persecution of Catholics.

Bonfire Night is still enthusiastically celebrated throughout Britain, though not everyone is wholly aware of the religious implications of the scarecrow-like 'guy' that is sent up in flames. At Lewes, however, the historical integrity of the Gunpowder Plot prevails. As well as bonfires, torch-lit parades, fancy-dress and huge fireworks displays, an effigy of the Pope gets the bonfire treatment as well, while mock cardinals are harried through the streets under a hail of good-natured abuse.

Lewes Bonfire Night is made even more impressive because the town boasts five 'bonfire societies', each of which vies with the others for the best displays. In recent years there have been protests about the perceived anti-Catholic nature of the papal pyre, but these have been countered by arguments that other effigies, including ones of Queen Elizabeth, George W. Bush and Winnie the Pooh have also been burned, suggesting that all bonfire guys are catholic with a small 'c' at least.

Fuller's Fabulous Follies

Brightling, Sussex

Down on the Downs round Brightling in Sussex there's a clutch of fabulous follies, courtesy of a 19th-century eccentric named 'Mad' Jack Fuller, a builder of fantastical landmarks that only money could buy.

Mad Jack was born in 1757 into a wealthy iron-founding family that made its fortune from slave-trading and producing guns for the British Navy. Jack was said to be larger than life – he weighed all of 127 kilograms (20 stone) when they levered him into his last 'folly', a large stone mausoleum, in the shape of a pyramid that still graces Brightling churchyard. Legend says that Jack's corpse was perched on an iron chair inside the tomb, a top hat was placed on his head and a bottle of claret and a roast chicken left at hand, ready for the Day of Reckoning. Never go anywhere on an empty stomach was Jack's motto.

He was certainly a great drinker. One of his most famous follies resulted from a drunken wager that he made with his boozing buddies one dark night. Jack claimed that, by day, he could see from his windows a good number of church steeples, including the steeple of Dallington Church. Large sums were placed on the bet, before most of the guests passed out.

At first light, Jack, still on his feet, realized that a couple of hills were in the way and that Dallington spire was not visible. Before his friends woke up he sent his workers to erect the top of a false steeple out of stones and clay. It was just visible above the horizon. He fooled his bleary-eyed friends, won his bet, and the false steeple, known as the Sugar Loaf or Fuller's Point, remains to this day.

Mad Jack Fuller's other fabulous follies include Brightling Needle – a 12-metre (40-foot) high obelisk built on the top of the hill at Brightling and used as a beacon point during the Napoleonic Wars – a small Greek temple, an observatory and a watch tower. Meanwhile, Jack waits patiently inside his pyramid...

BELOW: ***The Great Beast, No 666 or the Wickedest Man in the World are some of the monikers happily adopted by Aleister Crowley, Satanist, sadist and sexual climber...***

The Great Beast

Hastings, Sussex

The 'wickedest man in the world' is an awesome title, but it was cherished by the self-proclaimed Satanist, magician and degenerate Aleister Crowley, (1875–1947). After a life of unbridled lust and outrage, the old devil ended up in rather straitened circumstances in a Hastings lodging house, where he finally gave up the ghost, wickedly undaunted.

Crowley came from a wealthy brewing family and followed the well-trodden path of late Victorian youths of intelligence and means. Unfortunately, he soon went off at an angle as an undergraduate at Cambridge, where the murky world of magic and mysticism took a grip of him.

Malignancy as much as mysticism soon got the better of Crowley. He had courage and spirit enough and was an accomplished, if unorthodox mountaineer, even setting off in 1921 to climb K2, or Mount Godwin-Austen, the world's second highest mountain. K2 soon brought him down to size on its formidable lower slopes. Crowley also scaled the vertical chalk cliffs of Beachy Head using an ice axe and ropes.

Crowley loved japes. He once wrote to a remote Scottish village on the pretext of being chairperson of a society for the protection of public morals, complaining that 'prostitution was highly conspicuous' in the village. When the appalled village elders wrote back, protesting that there was not a prostitute within miles of their deeply religious community, Crowley replied, tartly, 'I meant conspicuous by its absence, you fools...'

Such escapades reflected a deeply cruel streak and before long Crowley was out of control, rampaging his way round the world, promoting his own brand of 'sex magic' and stuffing himself and his acolytes full of drugs. He styled himself the Great Beast and adopted the satanic number 666 before establishing a commune on Sicily that soon attracted several bewildered sons and daughters of wealthy families. Most were sadly damaged already and were soon destroyed under Crowley's spell. Animal sacrifices, sexual shenanigans, drug abuse and suicide were the order of the commune's day and soon established Crowley as irretrievably evil and probably mad. His activities supplied the tabloids of the day with lurid copy.

Crowley was hopelessly addicted to heroin, although his formidable constitution saw him into his seventies. A perverse romanticism still clings to his name, mainly among a few rebellious young. 'Do what thou wilt shall be the whole of the Law' was Crowley's mantra. Death finally obliged.

ABOVE: ***'Now listen carefully. I'll only bellow this once...' A town crier in fine voice.***

LARGING IT LOUDLY

Hastings, Sussex

'Oyez! Oyez!' You heard it here first; town criers were the original anchor-persons. The practice of using a big-voiced local (with apologies to newscasters everywhere) to shout out public announcements probably goes back to Ancient Greece, and before that to the loudmouthed village gossip of the Stone Age; but the first town criers seem to have arrived in Britain with the conquering Normans in the 11th century. They would stride about town, ringing a bell and calling 'Oyez!' – Old French for 'Hear Ye' – and delivering official proclamations in a booming baritone to the sullen and largely illiterate population.

As literacy levels improved and commercial printing evolved as a means of communication, the need for town criers diminished. As with so many other worthwhile items, however, Britain has managed to hang on to this theatrical and colourful tradition and today there are about 200 towns in the country with official town criers, who take part in ceremonial occasions and help to promote local tourism. Modern town criers wear the traditional robes and three-cornered hat of the handsome official costume that was first introduced during the 17th century.

The National Town Crier's Contest – to find the loudest and most stentorian voiceover – takes place in Hastings each October as part of Hastings Week. The 'week' commemorates the Norman Conquest of 1066 and celebrates the kind of essential contradiction that entirely characterizes British eccentricity, by lasting for nine days.

London & Kent

London and its adjoining county of Kent define Britain in many ways. This is the famous South-east, the bridgehead to mainland Europe and a region that has always attracted people from all parts of Britain. It is the seat of government and a powerhouse of trade and commerce, a region with an exotic architectural heritage; from medieval castles and 18th-century neo-classical buildings to a futuristic giant wheel on the banks of the Thames. London shines with cosmopolitan style and creativity. Yet amid the sometimes frantic pace of modern life, the city and its hinterland still harbour the eccentric and the unexpected; from a village vibrant with ghosts to people who dress in pearl-peppered suits or who go for a mid winter dip in the freezing waters of Hyde Park's Serpentine Lake.

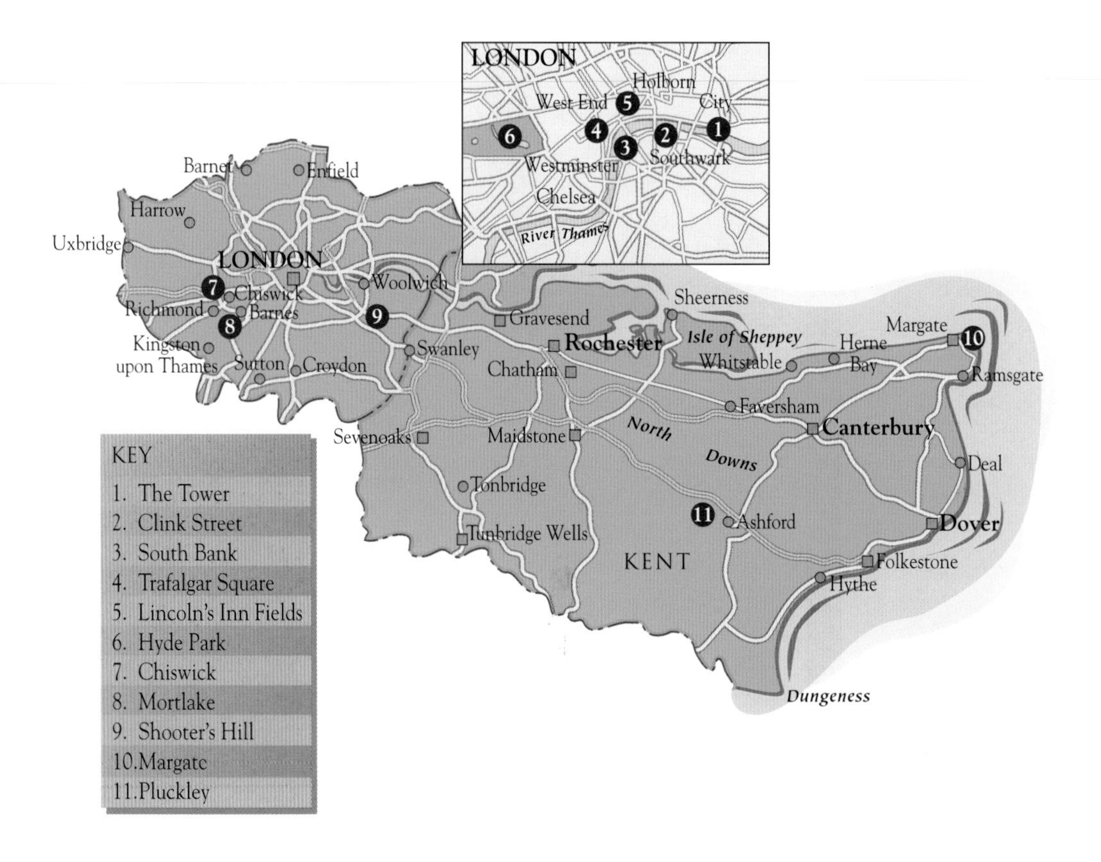

Caves, Clinks, Ghosts & Graves

Towering Times & Rare Ravens

The Tower, London

The Tower of London merges the dignity of history with some uniquely eccentric events. At exactly 9.53pm each evening, the Chief Yeoman Warder of the Tower marches out by the light of a lantern. He carries the Queen's Keys in his hand and he walks slowly toward the Bloody Tower past sentries and guards presenting arms. On the way the Chief Warder, resplendent in the famous Beefeater dress, closes and locks the doors of the Middle Tower and the Byward Tower; he then returns to the archway that leads into the Bloody Tower, where a sentry orders him to halt.

'Who goes there?' the sentry barks.
'The Keys,' answers the Chief Warder.
'Whose Keys?'
'Queen Elizabeth's Keys.'
'Pass Queen Elizabeth's Keys,' comes the order. 'All's well.'

The Chief Warder is then confronted by the Night Guard, whose sword-wielding officer calls, 'Guard and Escort, present Arms'; to which the Chief Warder raises his bonnet and declares, 'God preserve Queen Elizabeth.'

'Amen!' the Guard replies, just as it chimes ten o'clock; whereupon a bugler sounds the Last Post.

This curious Ceremony of the Keys has been carried

PREVIOUS PAGE: ***Pretty pictures inspired by the Tower of London's Changing of the Guard.***

LEFT: ***Casting light on the Tower of London, a place of dark despair, dark deeds and dark corners, yet imbued with English history and tradition.***

out for over 700 years and is believed to date from a time when the Tower was not only a royal residence and prison but the home of the Crown Jewels. Add to all of this historic security the alarm call of the Tower's famous ravens. There are seven of these wonderful birds, all with thoroughly odd names: Hardey, Thor, Odin, Gwyllum, Cedric, Hugine and Munin. Their wings are clipped, but not cruelly so. It is done to make sure they do not stray too far, although one raven did make it to a nearby pub. He was, inevitably, called Grog.

A Clinker of a Clink

Clink Street, London

Preaching about the torments of hell was easy-peasy for the Bishop of Winchester; he had his very own earthbound prison to match the worst evocations of hellfire. Now, you can visit the Clink Museum – a delightfully gruesome reconstruction of the Bishop's Clink Prison, in Clink Street, near Tower Bridge – on a carefree day out in London.

Bishops of Winchester had owned prisons of one sort or another since AD 860, and when a 12th-century incumbent built a chapel and mansion at Southwark in London in 1107, he gave orders for a gaol to be established in the grounds.

The Bishop's Prison was the original Clink – from which the slang term for prisons in general was taken. How the name itself originated is anyone's guess, but it may have echoed the deathly clink-clunk sound of a cell door slamming shut. Chapel, mansion and gaol were completed in 1144, and the Clink was soon full of tormented souls.

Religious sadism may have prompted the idea for the Clink – there was nothing like the real-time suffering of others to make the godly glad, but bishops of the day were nothing if not shrewd investors. The Bishop of Winchester was on a winner all round; the government paid him a fee per prisoner. Men and women were at least segregated, but not from each other's howls of agony as the bishop's bullies laid on the rack, the wheel, the crusher, the flesh hook, the scold's bridle and a host of vile instruments, too awful to mention.

In the 15th century, Henry VII ordered the imprisoning of priests who committed any form of adultery, incest and general fornication; the Clink was soon packed. Some years later Henry VIII legalized the awful punishment of boiling in oil for women who had murdered their husbands; there was apparently no equivalent fate for husbands who chopped off the heads of their wives.

ABOVE: ***London's Clink Museum portrays the dreadful days of genuine clinkery when Church and State considered cruelty to be 'normal'.***

The original Clink was destroyed long ago, but today it has been replicated as a delightfully gruesome museum, all dark and gloomy, lit by flickering candles, with waxwork models of inmates and eerie groans issuing from the darker reaches. You can even try on a ball and chain – if you haven't got one already...

Keeping an Eye on London

South Bank, London

Fairgrounds may have their big wheels, but the London Eye is a whale of a wheel. The enormous Eye, complete with its viewpoint gondolas, stands on the banks of the Thames and is a truly heroic feat of engineering. Commissioned to celebrate the Millennium, the London Eye was one of a coincidental trio of major installations of the period. The others were the infamous Millennium Dome at Greenwich, doomed, rather than domed, to never fill its own vacuum, and the stylish Blade of Light bridge that linked the St Paul's side of the River Thames with the Tate Modern on the river's South Bank. The bridge soon became a kind of trampoline, or wobbly castle, as the weight and footfalls of its first users set up a truly wonderful wobble, since sorted by old-fashioned dampers. Only the London Eye rose above Britain's Millennium muddle.

The Eye's statistics are eye-openers. The foundations alone required 3400 tons of concrete and 44 concrete piles, each 33 metres (108 feet) long. The structure itself is three times as high as Tower Bridge and four times the diameter of St Paul's Cathedral, and has a total weight of 1700 tons – equivalent to 250 London buses.

The wheel had to be assembled in a horizontal position and then winched into place. Naturally, the pessimistic British keened and moaned Cassandra-like in the background and, sure enough, erection was not accomplished at the first attempt. The Eye was sponsored by British Airways, whose rival Richard Branson – he of Virgin Atlantic and a Bognor Birdman to boot – organized a cheeky flyover stunt with a banner of the prone wheel bearing the rude slogan 'BA can't get it up!'

At the second attempt they certainly did and the Eye rose majestically into place, transforming London's skyline. The Eye opened for business in the first year of the new century. It can carry up to 15,000 passengers a day, yet needs only 500 kw of power to revolve. From the gliding gondolas you have a superb view of the capital and on clear days you can see as far as the dawn of the next millennium.

Pearls Aplenty

Trafalgar Square, London

Pearls aplenty are on show at London's Trafalgar Square on the first Sunday in October each year. That's when the city's famous Pearly Kings and Queens gather for their annual Harvest Festival at the church of St Martin's-in-the-Field.

The Pearlies' fascinating pearl-studded garb harks back, allegedly, to the arrival, in 1860s' London, of a big cargo of pearl-buttons from Japan. It wasn't long before an inventive local stall-holder, or 'costermonger' as they were then known, stitched a few pearl buttons round the seams of his waistcoat and his wide-bottomed trousers. The costers were known as Flash Boys because of it. There's nothing new under the flashlight of fashion.

The style caught on, but the full pearl jacket of today's Pearly Kings and Queens was developed by a Londoner called Henry Croft. Born in 1862, Henry was brought up in an orphanage and began work, aged 13, as a street sweeper and rat catcher.

Henry had a charitable streak and he began to collect alms, not least for his old orphanage. He hit on the idea of making a very flash pearly suit to give himself some profile and spent weary nights covering a suit with pearls. His first be-pearled appearance was at a local carnival where the extraordinary suit was an instant success. By the time Henry died in 1930 he is said to have raised £5000 for numerous hospitals and churches; a huge sum in today's terms.

Henry Croft attracted a following of Pearly people and soon most London boroughs had a Pearly tribe, each with an elected King and Queen. The magnificent suits, hats and dresses of today's remaining Pearlies have been handed down along with hereditary titles. The designs represent mystical and fertility symbols as well as stars, moons, suns, diamonds and flowers. Each outfit can have as many as 30,000 buttons and can weigh as much as 30 kilograms (66 pounds).

BELOW: ***Eye! Eye! London! The millennium majesty of the London Eye, a capital landmark for the 21st century.***

ABOVE: ***The Soane Museum is a fantastic collection of art works and artefacts as well as being an architectural showpiece, reflecting Sir John Soane's achievements.***

Strange Soane's

Lincoln's Inn Fields, London

The 18th-century architect, Sir John Soane, had a great line on lines, and his mastery of dimension, light and space was matched by a grand eccentricity of taste. The legacy is his Soane Museum in London's Lincoln's Inn Fields. The museum is one of the capital's most engaging attractions.

Sir John Soane was born in 1753 and was the son of a bricklayer. He became a distinguished architect, designed the Bank of England and was Professor of Architecture at the Royal Academy. Soane travelled in Italy, where he absorbed a host of cultural influences.

Soane built himself a house in Lincoln's Inn Fields, shaping its interior to his remarkable tastes, especially through the emphasis of domed spaces, arches and clerestories. Not content with architectural artistry, Sir John filled his house with splendid paintings that include Hogarth's marvellous *Rake's Progress*, as well as sculpture and furniture. The basement of the house replicates Roman catacombs and other rooms remain as they were during Sir John's occupancy. After his wife died in 1815, Soane continued to live in the house but encouraged its use as a kind of resource centre and library.

He was said to be bitterly disappointed with the behaviour of his two sons, and seems to have been determined that what he had created should go to the nation and to those who wished to better their minds. In 1833, a year after he had been knighted, he established his house as a museum by Act of Parliament and it has remained so ever since, an exhilarating experience for everyone. It can be visited, for free, any day except Monday.

The Serpentine Shiver

Hyde Park, London

Stroll by Hyde Park's famous Serpentine Lake any Saturday morning at 8 am and you'll spot the mightily brave Serpentine Swimming Club, a group of redoubtable people who keep up the custom of splashing their way across the slithery-slathery depths, even in the dead of winter.

The Serpentine swim-centrics are not the only British bulldogs to brave the less than temperate waters of the island. There are outdoor daily swimmers all over the country, from Penzance in Cornwall and brisk Brighton in Sussex to the chilly wastes of the nippy North Sea at Scarborough in Yorkshire. Even further north, in Scotland, there are devoted all-year-round swimmers who will tell you that it gets warmer the more you do it.

There's something particularly fascinating about London's Serpentine Swimmers, however. A man-made lake in London's enormous Hyde Park is not the most inviting stretch of water, even in the height of summer. But the Serpentiners are at it even when hell freezes over; they just chop through the ice and plunge in. On Christmas Day, the Serpentine Club stages a 90 -metre race for the Peter Pan Cup, a competition that has been running for more than 125 years.

Anyone keen to indulge in year-round dips is strongly advised to start the process in the company of experienced swimmers, preferably during the warmer

summer months to build up resilience for those ice-breaking winter mornings.

ABOVE: *London's Serpentine Lake in Hyde Park is the venue for a remarkable band of regular bathers.*

A Chiswick Charmer

Chiswick, London

The 18th-century Chiswick House is said to be the finest Palladian villa in Britain, although it is less of a villa and more of a Temple of Art. Chiswick's marvellous eccentricity lies in a triumph of design over function that created sumptuous reception rooms but eschewed such domestic essentials as a kitchen; there was a fine wine cellar all the same.

The designer of Chiswick House, the gifted Earl of Burlington, created his villa as a gathering place for artists and writers rather than as a home. Burlington was an enthusiastic patron of Palladian architecture. He had spent a year in Italy and had been entranced by the work of the 16th-century architect Andrea Palladio, a major figure of the Renaissance who based his architectural ideas on Roman classicism, and especially on the design of Roman temples.

Lord Burlington was captivated by Palladio's Villa Capra outside the Italian town of Vicenza. A main theme of Palladianism was the central domed hall and it is this feature that dominates the design of Chiswick House. Burlington did not stint on the villa's surroundings either. Palladianism demanded context and the garden of Chiswick House is a lavish expression of the classical ideal.

The cream of 18th-century society trooped to Chiswick House. Lord Burlington supported a host of writers, poets, painters and musicians, from Jonathan Swift and Alexander Pope to the composer Handel. British royalty and Russian tsars visited, as did British prime ministers

'I LIKE THE FACT THAT THERE'S NO REASON FOR DOING IT. IT'S COLD AND COMPLETELY BANANAS...'

Outdoor swimmer on Christmas Day

and the American presidents John Quincy Adams and Thomas Jefferson. Today, Chiswick House and its gardens are open to the public daily from April to October.

SAHARAN SEPULCHRE IN SUBURBIA

Mortlake, London

Deep in the heart of suburban London, in the leafy graveyard of the Church of St Mary Magdalene at Mortlake, lies an exotic Arabian tent – made entirely of marble and stone. Utterly lifelike in its subtle folds and drapes, the 'tent' is in fact a mausoleum, the grave of the fantastic 19th-century explorer and adventurer, Sir Richard Burton. It's a magnificent, eccentric memorial to a magnificent eccentric.

Richard Burton was one of the Western world's greatest travellers. He was born in the seaside resort of Torquay, Devon, in 1821; but the sea did not detain him long and he turned inland in a very big way. He also became fluent in over two dozen languages and dialects.

In 1853, Burton travelled to Cairo, Suez and the holy cities of Medina and Mecca, always disguised as a native and speaking fluent Arabic. (He would have been executed immediately had he been discovered to be European.) Among his other achievements, Burton went looking for the source of the White Nile with John Hanning Speke; he and Speke were the first Europeans to set eyes on Lake Tanganyika.

Burton was appointed consul in Trieste in 1872 and it was during his long service there that he wrote several remarkable books, including his translation of the 16 volumes of *The Tales of the Arabian Nights.* His candid revelations about the lushness of Arabian sexuality shocked many of his contemporaries. His wife, Isabel Arundel Gordon, burned the manuscript of his translation of *The Perfumed Garden* because she was afraid that its explicit descriptions of sexuality would ruin Burton's reputation.

ABOVE LEFT: ***Urns in the grounds and impeccable classicism in the buildings; Chiswick House is a triumph of architectural taste over function.***

LEFT: ***Explorer Richard Burton's magnificent mausoleum at Mortlake. Is it sepulchral stone or Saharan silk?***

Burton was knighted by Queen Victoria, who may have been secretly amused. He died in Trieste in 1890; his wish was that he should be buried in the desert, but Isabel compromised ingeniously by creating the famous Mortlake Sheikh's Tomb, complete with tent. The tent even has a metal ladder, so that you can climb up and peer through a window in the roof to where Burton and his devoted wife lie in their coffins surrounded by memorials of his expeditions.

A Pirate Policeman's Castle

Shooter's Hill, London

High on Shooter's Hill in Castlewood Park, south-east London, stands Severndroog Castle, its name alone making a bizarre link between the city and the exotic coast of Malabar in India. The castle is really a tower and, three-sided and three-storeyed, has all the gloomy delights of 18th-century Gothic, including hexagonal turrets. It is a good 12 metres (9 feet) higher in altitude than St Paul's Cathedral.

Severndroog Castle was built as a memorial to Sir William James, an 18th-century sea captain who policed the pirate-haunted Indian coast during the heyday of the British East India Company. James first went to sea on coastal vessels, but later sailed to the West Indies, before joining the British East India Company in 1747. He became a sea captain in the private army that the company used in order to keep an iron grip on its investments. Pirates along the coast of Malabar were a major problem and William James was put in charge of anti-pirate patrols.

A mightily feared pirate chief, with the wonderful name Tollagee Angria was based in the island fortress of Severndroog, from where he masterminded his campaigns. In 1755, Captain James attacked Severndroog, destroying the fortress and putting paid to Tollagee Angria and his gang. In their skinflint way, the East India Company gave the good captain £100 as a token of his victory; but the canny James later made his fortune harrying the French who were trying to establish their own trading posts along the coast of Malabar. Such was the anarchy of Imperial rule in the good old days.

RIGHT: *Severndroog Castle on Shooter's Hill reflects a typical celebration of Britain's Imperial past when a favoured few had money to spare for oddball memorials.*

ABOVE: ***18th-century cave cartoons at Margate Caves may, or may not, have erased prehistoric tool marks.***

William James eventually became a director of the East India Company and a Fellow of the Royal Society. He died in 1784 and, soon after, his wife paid to have the tower built at Shooter's Hill in memory of Sir William and his victory at Severndroog. From the castle there are clear views over the Thames, up which no pirate ships – other than those of the British, laden with booty – ever dared steal.

QUIRKY CAVES

Margate, Kent

Down in the seaside resort of Margate are two mysterious artificial cave systems whose origins are unknown – although they have been explained variously as being ancient burial chambers, dungeons, smugglers' dens and Georgian follies.

Known as Margate Cave and Shell Cave, the systems comprise a series of tunnels and galleries in the chalk hillside of Cliftonville. They are said to have been discovered only in the late 18th century by the gardener of a wealthy eccentric, Francis Foster, who had built himself a house at Cliftonville.

Foster's gardener realized that there were sizeable cavities in the hillside and an entrance was cut to gain better access. Tool marks on the walls might have offered archaeologists evidence of when the caves were created, but the wall surfaces were smoothed over when a local artist painted several murals.

Creation of the caves has been variously ascribed to the Phoenicians, the Romans and the Saxons. Roman origin is feasible as the Romans' certainly quarried chalk for a number of uses. The most intriguing suggestion is that the caves were secretly carved out by Francis Foster himself, although what he would have done with all that chalk has not been satisfactorily explained.

Ghostly Gridlock

Pluckley, Kent

ABOVE: ***Ghosts are gridlocked round Pluckley's Church of St Nicholas and around the village in general.***

In the Kent village of Pluckley there seems to be more of a ghostly gridlock than anywhere else in Britain. Pluckley is enshrined in the Guinness Book of Records as being 'the most haunted village in England', because of its tally of 16 recorded wraiths. They probably have a rota system to regulate the traffic.

What makes Pluckley's phantoms so active may reflect the 500-year tenure of the local manor by the Dering family, many of whom lie in the burial vaults of the local church of St Nicholas. Their restless shades fidget and rattle, while mysterious lights flicker inside the church and knocking sounds are a regular accompaniment.

Out in the churchyard the ghosts of two Dering ladies hold sway. One is the Red Lady, the other the White Lady. The former laments the death of her baby; the other is simply out on parole from a secure series of Russian doll coffins in which her husband placed her body, hoping to preserve her fleshly beauty.

Pluckley Phantasmagoria does not stop at church and churchyard, however. Throughout the village and its neighbourhood, the ghosts of lovelorn ladies, an executed monk, a drowned labourer, a suicidal schoolmaster, a miller and a gypsy woman, all hang out. A highwayman, stabbed to death by pursuers, is said to haunt the aptly named Frit, or Fright Corner.

Meanwhile, a ghostly horse and carriage glides along country roads and there have been reports of a phantom pipe and drum band. Poltergeists rattle the cutlery and the empty glasses and rearrange the furniture at the local Black Horse Inn – where many of Pluckley's ghost stories may well originate, among the other spirits.

Essex, Suffolk & Norfolk

The counties of Essex, Suffolk and Norfolk make up the great humped shoulder of eastern England, known for centuries as East Anglia. This is where the milder south of the country gives way to the brisker north and where land and sea intermingle on a daily basis as North Sea tides come and go across the low-lying landscape. There is a remarkable remoteness about many parts of the region; life moves at a steady pace and the old values of English rural life still hold sway. This is Olde England in the truest sense, a world of great individuality where the robust traditions of English eccentricity are upheld in everything from Morris dancing to mud racing and where you'll find engaging quirkiness and colourful artistry in village signposts and at the world's finest teapot museum.

GORN
OLLIES

Morris Men, Mudlarks, Teapots & Towers

MUDLARKING

Maldon, Essex

In midwinter Maldon, they have a unique way of welcoming in the New Year – they go mud racing. There's nothing quite so all-embracing as the mousse-like mud of a tidal estuary. When the tide is in it all looks fairly fresh, but at low tide what you have is a perfect purée of richly pungent sludge. It's also very, very cold – the ideal venue for a race track.

Maldon's Mud Race is all for good causes, of course, and various charities benefit from the mudlarking of over 500 entrants each year. The race takes place on the first weekend after Christmas Day and is organized by the local Rotary and Lions Club. The course is a mere 365 metres (1197 feet); but when it's along the bed of the River Crouch, all black mud and slime, the conditions underfoot control the level of running – or the crawling, for that matter. The head of the field gets the firmest footing. Stragglers end up in treacle. Competitors can wear fancy dress; some wear wet suits, but the meeting of mud and neoprene turns mud racing into skid-surfing. The bravest simply thong it.

The idea for this unique event is said to have originated some years ago when one local worthy bet another that he wouldn't eat his Christmas dinner on a mud bank. The challenger lost the bet and the mud race developed.

Whatever its origins, there's no doubt that the Mud Race has put Maldon on the whacky world map. Entrants come from all over Britain and from as far afield as Italy and Japan. Nothing quite like it for cooling the blood.

MERRY MORRIS MEN

Thaxted, Essex

No matter how eccentric Morris dancing may seem, there's something eternally fascinating about the stick-clashing, bell-babbling, kerchief-waving rhythms of this strange old English custom. The Scots dance on swords and Morris dancers stick to sticks – with bells on. Each year, on the last weekend in May, there's a huge gathering of Morris dancers at Thaxted known as the Thaxted Ring Meeting.

Morris dancing was not always seen as benevolent. Grim-faced old puritan Philip Stubbes called Morris the 'Devil's Dance' in his *Anatomie of Abuses* (1583). No one knows where the dance originates. It may hark back to ancient ritual that is reflected in the processional form, symbolic movement and circular routines of today's Morris dancing. By Elizabethan times Morris was already regarded as an ancient custom, deserving of mention by no less than Shakespeare, and by James I in his *Book of Sports.* For enthusiasts such dances were

'MORRISMEN DID MARTCH THIS HEATHEN COMPANY TOWARDS THE CHURCH AND CHURCHYARDS, THEIR PYPERS PYPING, THE DRUMMERS THUNDERING, THEIR STUMPES DANCING, THEIR BELLES JYNGLING, THEIR HAND-KERCHEEFES FLUTTERING ABOUT THEIR HEADS LIKE MADDE MEN.'

Philip Stubbes **(Anatomie of Abuses, *1583*)**

believed to bring luck and to ward off evil.

The name Morris is the real mystery. One theory suggests that it is a corruption of the word 'Moorish', deriving from dances brought to England from Muslim countries by Crusaders – the name does resemble the word *morisco,* which was the term applied to Muslims who had converted to Christianity in medieval Spain. The use of castanets in flamenco dancing is thus seen as a possible precursor of the bells and clacking sticks of Morris dancing. Another theory is that Morris dancing may have borrowed aspects of its dress from the costumes and bells worn by court jesters.

Whatever the theories, Morris dancing remains an intriguing and endearing custom. There are many events throughout the summer at which Morris dancers perform, but Thaxted's Ring Meeting is one of the most colourful and entertaining of all.

ABOVE: *The original 'red-brick university' of Freston Tower, where Ellen de Freston rose steadily from floor to floor in pursuit of academic excellence.*

PREVIOUS PAGE AND OPPOSITE: *The mighty Morris or 'Moorish'? The origins of Morris dancing are claimed by some to derive from the dances of North Africa or of Muslim Spain.*

RED BRICK RUMINATIONS

River Orwell, Suffolk

The original 'red-brick' university could well have been Freston Tower, a six-storey tower above the estuary of the River Orwell, south of Ipswich.

The tower was built by Lord de Freston in the 1560s. Its purpose in those uncertain times may have been as a lookout for keeping watch on shipping on the Orwell, but a more eccentric tale suggests that it was used as a bizarre school for Lord de F's daughter, Ellen.

The tower is a fairly simple square building in red brick. There are polygonal angle buttresses that end as little turrets at each corner of a parapet, which has a small observatory lantern. Some claim that Freston Tower is England's oldest folly, although the definition of a folly as being essentially useless hardly fits the strictly pragmatic purpose of the tower. Each floor of Lord de Freston's Tower measures 3 x 3.5 metres (10 x 11 feet) and each room was designated as a study for Educating Ellen under the following strict regime:

The Lower room to charity from 7 to 8 o'clock
The Second to working tapestry from 9 to 10
The Third to music from 10 to noon
The Fourth to painting from 12 to 1
The Fifth to Literature from 1 to 2
The Sixth to astronomy at even.

By the time she staggered to the top beneath the weight of all that brain-battering, poor Ellen must have been seeing stars anyway. Freston Tower is now a letting property of the Landmark Trust.

Peter Pan's Wendy Water House

Thorpeness, Suffolk

The Peter Pan House in the mock-Tudor village of Thorpeness is also known as the House in the Clouds. It's a fitting name, given that the house once played the dual role of dwelling and water tower. Tenants of its lower rooms lived with a potential cloudburst of 30,000 gallons of water just above their heads.

This intriguing building was the inspiration of the splendidly named Glencairn Stuart Ogilvie, whose family owned land around the small village of Thorpe, north of Aldeburgh. Ogilvie inherited the property in 1903 and set out to create a development of holiday homes around an artificial system of waterways and little islands, known as The Meare. The Ogilvie family were close friends of J M Barrie, the creator of Peter Pan, and the islands on the Meare are all named after characters in Barrie's famous book.

Supplying water for the development required a water tower, and Ogilvie and his architect came up with an ingenious scheme for merging the practical with the Peter Pannery. They installed the tower, then disguised it by converting the bottom half into a five-storey dwelling. The tank was made to look like a clapboard house, complete with pitched roof, false windows and a chimney. Tenants were unconcerned about the watery attic and its gurglings, and several were enchanted by the place. Ogilvie had called the tower, The Home of Peter Pan, but one of his tenants wrote a poem about the tower entitled 'The House in the Clouds' and the name stuck.

The House in the Clouds is no longer used as a water tower, but it survives in its house-like form. Thousands of people visit Thorpeness each year and you can hire Canadian-style canoes and other small boats for a jaunt on the delightful Meare.

Norfolk has another splendid water tower that is now a dwelling. This is Appleton Water Tower at Sandringham, a handsome building that dates from 1877 and is now leased and let by the Landmark Trust.

LEFT: ***Woter lot of water! The delightful Peter Pan House or the 'House in the Clouds' at Thorpeness. The upper storey disguises an old water tank.***

Bristol Bizarre

Horringer, Suffolk

The eccentric but enchanting Ickworth House in Horringer was the inspiration of the equally eccentric 4th Earl of Bristol, Frederick Hervey. He was also the Bishop of Derry.

The Hervey family had a foothold in England from the days of William the Conqueror. They were very odd Normans. Not much is known about the early Herveys, but the strain matured into high quirkiness by the time of Lord John Hervey (1696–1743). He was known as Lord Fanny, not least because of his habit of wearing heavy rouge and because of his male lovers.

The 3rd Earl of Bristol, Augustus Hervey, was a naval captain and a notorious drinker and seducer, who fulfilled the dictum of having a girl in every port and a port in every girl. The modern Herveys were just as dangerously eccentric. The 6th Marquess of Bristol, who died in 1985, was an unsuccessful gun-runner, robber and playboy. His son, the 7th Marquess, died in 1999 after a life of drug abuse and profligate spending of the family fortune.

Frederick the 4th Earl's earlier perambulations through Italy during the 18th century were on a similar scale of outrageous behaviour, the least of which was riding around dressed in nightgown and cap in a carriage with a trio of tarts. He was once imprisoned in a castle. The earl conceived Ickworth as being a suitable repository for his formidable collection of paintings. Building work began at Ickworth during the Earl's lifetime, but Bristol was caught out in Italy by the Napoleonic Wars and promptly died in 1803. It was not until 1826 that serious work began on completing Ickworth House.

Today Ickworth House and its park and gardens are in the care of the National Trust. The main feature of the House is the oval rotunda, which is over 30 metres (98 feet) high. Curved corridors lead off from it to the wings, one of which contains sculpture, the other paintings, including works by Titian, Velazquez and Gainsborough. The 4th Earl's superb collection of Georgian silver is also on display. House, park and garden can be visited.

BELOW: ***Ickworth House, the gloriously eccentric creation of the gloriously eccentric 4th Earl of Bristol.***

ABOVE: *Towers with a tall story. The twin towers of Wymondham's parish church are the result of a row between monks and parishioners.*

A Towering Tiff

Wymondham, Norfolk

Two very similar towers grace either end of the parish church at Wymondham, tokens of a bizarre medieval dispute over who should rule the religious roost.

Originally founded as a Benedictine priory in 1107, Wymondham Abbey had a cruciform shape with a central tower and two smaller towers. The view of its secular founder was that the church should be shared by the monks and townspeople. The monks had other ideas; they petitioned Pope Innocent IV for sole authority, but in a rather splendid Judgement of Solomon, the Pope ruled that the monks should control one half of the church and the townspeople the other. The monks had the central tower, the townsfolk the two smaller ones.

This arrangement worked fairly well for many years, until 1411 when the monks replaced their tower with a much smarter one. Monks and locals then had a ding-dong row about whose tower should house the church bells. The monks blocked off the entrance to the locals' tower with a wall. The locals knocked the wall down and then blocked off the monks' entrance to the church. Then things took a really nasty turn when the locals kidnapped the prior.

The Archbishop of Canterbury was finally called in to knock heads together and ruled that the church should remain divided, but gave the locals permission to knock down their two small towers and to replace them with a single tower. At first the townspeople aimed to make their tower much higher than the monks' tower, but they seem to have settled for equal height.

Today the bulk of the old abbey buildings are gone and Wymondham's fine church has a traditional shape; except for the towers at either end, their backs turned towards each other.

Signing Up for a Sense of Pride

Swaffham, Norfolk

Most towns and villages in Britain have deeply dull signposts on their outskirts, although many make the effort and install something slightly more interesting than bland letters against an even blander background. But when it comes to village signposts, Norfolk is streets ahead of the rest of Britain.

Norfolk's unique tradition of colourful and creative signs had its source in the early years of the 20th century when King Edward VII encouraged the creation of individual signs to add colour and a sense of identity to the many villages near the Royal Sandringham Estate.

The signs were first manufactured in a workshop known as the Queen's Carving School, but in 1929 a Swaffham man, Harry Carter, who was art and woodwork master at a local school, carved a sign for Swaffham out of English oak. The sign was such a success that Harry was signed up by other villages. His signs were painstakingly carved and sometimes took as long as six months to complete. All were painted and decorated with gold leaf, with each one depicting a local legend to do with its host village. When Harry Carter died in 1983 there were over 200 of his signs gracing the region's villages.

Harry Carter's signs are distinctive folk art and have a delightful originality. His sign for the town of

Dereham spans the width of the High Street. Other Carter signs of note include the Boy Scout sign at beautiful Anmer village. The sign was commissioned by the Norfolk Scouts' Association and bears the figure of a scout on one side. Always mindful of East Anglian history, Harry included a Roman centurion on the other side.

At the tiny hamlet of Babingley near Sandringham, the Carter sign commemorates St Felix, who is said to have founded at Babingley in AD 600 the first Christian church in East Anglia. Legend tells of how Felix was shipwrecked in the nearby river, now a mere trickle. He was rescued by a colony of beavers and in turn appointed the head beaver as his bishop. You need to hang on tight to this kind of story; but it's all there on Harry Carter's Babingley signpost – St Felix below, Bishop Beaver above.

ABOVE: ***Harry Carter turned out scores of signs for Norfolk villages. This one of a Roman centurion commemorated the area's association with Roman occupation.***

A Davidson Come to Judgement

Stiffkey, Norfolk

The Reverend Harold Davidson plunged early into the lion's den of controversy. He made it his life's work to save 'fallen women' and estimated that he had saved 1000 souls.

In 1905, Reverend Davidson became rector of Stiffkey on the Norfolk coast, just east of Wells-next-the-sea and not far from Great Snoring and Little Snoring. These are names you could not make up. Unchallenged by the demands of his rural parish, and, allegedly, cuckolded by his wife, Davidson embarked on a mission to save souls. He abandoned Stiffkey on Monday mornings and spent the week in London on 'missionary work'.

At first the crusading rector spread his net wide to catch the fallen of both sexes and of all ages; but increasingly he concentrated on attractive young women. 'I like to catch them young' was Harold's dictum. Davidson hung around tea shops chatting up waitresses, but was eventually banned from most premises. He turned his attention more directly to prostitutes and 'adopted' a number of them; in turn they treated him kindly enough until his notoriety proved marketable and some flogged their stories to the tabloids of the day. Several of Davidson's young ladies stayed at the Stiffkey rectory and, allegedly, plied their trade in hedgerow and hayrick. This was the final straw for influential locals who demanded the rector's dismissal after he failed to turn up to an Armistice Day service.

In 1932, Davidson was tried by a consistory court of the diocese of Norwich on charges of adultery and with consorting with 'women of loose character for immoral purposes'. He did a fair job of defending himself, until the prosecution produced a photograph featuring him with a near-naked teenage girl.

Defrocked, poor Davidson fell further than most, although he was remembered fondly by many of the

ABOVE: ***Tea for more than two at Norwich Castle's Teapot Museum, where the Great British Tea Party is celebrated in style.***

admirable parishioners of Stiffkey as a man of true humanity. He spent some time in a barrel on Blackpool promenade charging twopence a view, but was prosecuted for obstructing the public highway. He then did a Variety act in music hall, before moving to Skegness, where he staged his act in a cage with a lion called Freddy. The act consisted mainly of Davidson denouncing the entire Church of England. The content didn't always go down well with the crowd. Or with Freddy either; although Davidson went down well. One night Freddy ate him.

Topping Teapots

Norwich, Norfolk

Tea is the British coffee. And even though more exotic beverages are making inroads on the Great British tea break, an infusion of the stimulating *Camellia sinensis* is the British answer to everything.

It is hardly surprising therefore that Britain has a museum celebrating the simple teapot, that iconic receptacle that dominated the domestic life of generations. The Twining Teapot Gallery is located in Norwich Castle and encompasses a collection of over 3000 pots, of which about 600 are on display. Most come from the private collections of enthusiasts.

The gallery tells the fascinating story of 300 years of tea and tea-potting since the first leaves came from China to Britain in 1650. Tea was initially an expensive luxury and the teapots of the 18th century were small but very costly artefacts whose sculpted designs aped the architectural classicism of the time.

The collection includes some delightful pieces, including Wedgewood pots in the shape of plump vegetables such as cabbage and cauliflower. There are also some splendidly creative modern pots, such as a Giant Queen Tea Pot that weighs 20 kilograms (44 pounds), and a pot shaped like a hand, the thumb being the spout and one of the fingers being the lid.

Helter-Skelter House

Potter Heigham, Norfolk

On the banks of a Broad, near Potter Heigham, stands a charming little house with a roof like an old-fashioned soldier's helmet, or a slightly squashed bowler hat. At first glance the building looks as if it might be a truncated windmill, which would be no surprise in Norfolk. But a closer look reveals that adjacent to the house are other similar buildings. All are sections of a helter-skelter tower that once graced the pier at Yarmouth and was a great favourite during the early years of the 20th century.

The Yarmouth helter-skelter fell out of favour and is believed to have been stored away somewhere in the depths of the town. Much later an imaginative house-hunter bought the lot and had the sections transported along the Broads as far as Potter Heigham. Here the middle section of the old tower was turned into a house, while the upper sections did service as storerooms.

Today the Helter-Skelter House is a holiday home; and it still entertains visually as much as it ever did as a carnival ride.

RIGHT: *Topped off with a tidy hat is the Helter Skelter House at Potter Heigham, where it adds a carnival atmosphere to the Norfolk Broads.*

Snail's Pace Race

Congham, Norfolk

Don't rush... it's a snail's pace race at the village of Congham every July, when the steady-as-she-goes snailocracy of world racing gather to compete, albeit sluggishly, for the honour of being world champion.

Competitors sport some fairly flash names. There's Linford Christie, Fat Boy Slime, Super Slug, the Slime Machine and the rather racy-sounding Silver Streak. Races are run over a 33-centimetre (12-inch) course. The current record, achieved in 1995 by a snail called Archie, stands at 2 minutes flat, which for Jeremy Clarkson's benefit is 0.0028 mph.

World Snail Racing has been a hugely popular event at the Congham village fete for over 30 years. Money raised goes to maintain the 13th-century St Andrew's Church and interest in snail racing shows no signs of slowing down.

Congham is located in an area noted for its high humidity, an essential feature of snail racing, given snails' love of damp conditions. Heat wave years are not conducive to a fast course, although a bit of judicious sprinkling of water on the course goes down a treat. About 200 snails are entered for a series of heats leading up to a grand final. Anyone can enter on the day as snails are available from the safe hands of long-standing snail trainer Neil Riseborough. Dedicated racers claim to coach their would-be champions with some intensity and say that affection is the secret of training a super snail. Small snails with small backpacks are naturally the best hope. The prize for the world champ is a silver tankard full of lettuce leaves.

Hertfordshire, Bedfordshire, Buckinghamshire, Cambridgeshire & Northamptonshire

Tucked away at the heart of England is a cluster of charming counties whose names evoke images of Britain at its rustic best. Those names are a mouthful at times; you can easily enunciate Herts, Beds and Bucks, but you need to take a run at getting your tongue round Cambridgeshire and Northamptonshire. These are the true hidden corners of England, filled with delightful villages and old houses. and enlivened here and there with eccentric buildings that ring the changes, from Gothic temple and Sham church to a cottage orné. The spirit of fascinating festival and crazy custom is alive and well in a world of straw bears, swans, Stilton cheese, Hellfire caves, and a tree cathedral.

Straw Bears, Stilton, Swans & Hellfire

A Classic Sham

Ayot St Lawrence, Hertfordshire

The pleasant village of Ayot St Lawrence is famous for its Shaw, its silkworm factory and its Sham. The Shaw was George Bernard of that ilk, playwright extraordinary – G.B.S. lived in Ayot St.Lawrence for 44 years. The silkworm factory functioned during the mid 20th century; the only one in England at the time; it produced church vestments. But Ayot's most fascinating feature is the Sham – a village church masquerading as a rather elegant Greek temple with Doric façade, colonnaded wings and small pavilions.

PREVIOUS PAGE: ***The Dashwood estate boasts a splendid mausoleum, built in 1765.***
BELOW: ***Sir Lionel Lyte's handsome Sham Church at Ayot St Lawrence was all front, with bare brick behind.***

The Sham church was the work of Sir Lionel Lyte, lord of the manor during the late 18th century. In the way of things Sir Lionel fancied building a church. Announcing the plan as being of benefit to the entire village, he began to demolish Ayot's existing, and rather handsome, Norman church. The local bishop stopped him, although some say the 'ruined' church was a purposeful piece of instant Heritage. The ruin survives, carefully preserved, opposite the village pub.

Sir Lionel's church survives also in all its classical glory. It has a splendid stuccoed front. This was because Sir Lionel could see that side from his own house. The body and back of the building is in unrendered brick

for the villagers to gaze at.

Sir Lionel is said to have included the pavilion wings, satisfyingly at arm's length from each other, as mausoleums for himself and his wife. Relations between them were not good and this was Sir Lionel's little architectural conceit. He was determined that the church, which had united the unhappy pair in life, would keep them well apart in death.

Woodland Worship

Whipsnade, Bedfordshire

Talking to trees is no bad thing and at Whipsnade in Bedfordshire, the remarkable Tree Cathedral means that you can pray to them as well.

The soaring spires, graceful arches and intricate mouldings of Gothic cathedrals are said to have derived from the imagery of ancient forests and their tracery of tall trees, arched boughs and leafy branches. The Tree Cathedral takes that concept to its literal conclusion. It's a full-sized cathedral complete with nave, transepts, chapels and cloisters made entirely from living trees.

The cathedral was the inspiration of local man E. K. Blythe in the 1930s after he was inspired by a visit to Liverpool Cathedral. Blythe was a veteran of the First World War, and while his monumental gardening project was never intended to be a real cathedral, his admirable intent was that it would foster faith, hope and reconciliation.

The types of tree used were chosen carefully for their shape and colour – stately, upright poplars for the pillars, cherry trees for the Easter Chapel, and Norway spruce for the Winter Chapel were just some of the species used. Blythe worked on his project throughout the 1930s, and the cathedral was finished by 1939, ironically at the outbreak of the Second World War.

During the war years the cathedral was understandably neglected and nature, in its Gothic way, began to take over. The trees became overgrown, and thorn and scrub invaded the aisles. After the war a long process of recreation began and this work is being continued by the National Trust, who now care for the site.

The Tree Cathedral has never been consecrated as a formal place of worship, but interdenominational services are held annually, and the cathedral can be visited throughout the year.

ABOVE: *Building altars in the field at Whipsnade's Tree Cathedral, where the sky passes for stained glass.*

Aping The Alps

Biggleswade, Bedfordshire

The Swiss Garden at Biggleswade is an enchanting example of the eccentric craze for the picturesque that swept through late 18th-century England.

This was the era of the Grand Tour, when wealthy Gap Year grandees set off from England for a ramble through mainland Europe, eagerly absorbing influences and acquiring ideas along the way.

These early tourists came home full of grand architectural dreams, the realization of which resulted in many a mansion and stately home. For others the dream was realized through the creation of picturesque ornamental gardens full of grottoes, follies and flourishes. The 'picturesque' was best defined as the transformation of landscape into a three-dimensional replica of a painting. One classic feature of the picturesque was the cottage orné, a 'rustic' thatched cottage with rough wooden planking for walls, deep Alpine eaves and carved weather-boarding. These fairy-tale features sprang up like surreal fungi amidst the planned woodlands and walkways of great estates.

The Swiss Garden dates from the 1820s and was the inspiration of Lord Ongley. A central feature is the Swiss chalet, a typical cottage orné which makes use of wood that has not been stripped of its bark. The 3.82 hectares (10 acres) of garden also feature a fern grotto and various other quaint items such as ornate bridges, little follies and pools, all amid trees, shrubbery and colourful flowers.

The Swiss Garden is open on Sundays throughout the year and daily from March to September.

ABOVE: ***A classic Cottage Orné commands the vista at Biggleswade's Swiss Garden.***

Gothic Grandiose

Stowe, Buckinghamshire

The grand Palladian mansion at Stowe, now a famous school, is enough to enchant anyone. But this famous old estate has in its extensive gardens a collection of fascinating and eccentric temples that complement the house. The remarkable Gothic Temple is one of the finest.

Stowe was the creation of the Temple family during the 18th century. The family's motto was *Templa quam dilecta*, 'How delightful art thy temples'. Nothing was going to temper the Temples' pride in their name.

The estate eventually thronged with follies, all with allegorical themes that celebrated the artistic and political ideals of the 18th-century Enlightenment. The Gothic Temple was said to reflect Sir Richard Temple (Lord Cobham)'s support for civil liberty; or, more precisely, the imagined ancestral liberties of Saxon England.

ABOVE: ***The Gothic Temple at Stowe was built in 1741 and is a perfect exemplar of 18th century Enlightenment married to a romantic nostalgia for the medieval period.***

The Gothic Temple is a startling and compelling building, triangular in shape, built of earthy ironstone and looking as if it had sprung ready-made from the earth itself. There are turrets at the three angles and all the rooms are circular. The central chamber has an exquisite vaulted ceiling, handsomely decorated with heraldic themes. It bears various mottoes, including the Temple family motto.

The building has been restored by the Landmark Trust and is available through the Trust as holiday accommodation.

Hellfire Happy

West Wycombe, Buckinghamshire

Sir Francis Dashwood must have done some heavy clubbing during his Grand Tour of Europe and the Ottoman Empire in the 18th century. Most modern clubbers are saints compared to the Hon. Dashwood. He was thrown out of Italy for his outrageous behaviour, which included setting about worshippers in Rome's Sistine chapel with a horse whip. They'd been simulating pious self-scourging when Sir Francis decided they needed a taste of the real thing.

Eventually, the Hon. Dashwood came home to West Wycombe in England and founded a Hellfire Club to indulge himself and 'a set of worthy, jolly fellows, happy disciples of Venus and Bacchus, who got together to celebrate women in wine'.

Hellfire was a generic name for a number of such good-time 'societies' that had tormented the pious for

'A SET OF WORTHY, JOLLY FELLOWS, HAPPY DISCIPLES OF VENUS AND BACCHUS'

John Wilkes, member of a 'Hellfire Club'

many years. Sir Francis and his friends dubbed themselves officially as Monks of Medmenham, or the Knights of St Francis. This was in the hope of passing off their outrageous activities as anti-Catholic mockery – an attitude that was popular with the establishment, although the 'monks' main habit involved them romping in and out of their habits with naked women on an altar.

The club usually met at Medmenham Abbey for dinner and drinks in the company of these 'ladies of a cheerful and lively disposition'. Notable monks included poets and writers, members of parliament, and other leading figures such as Benjamin Franklin and John Wilkes. According to Wilkes the group 'plucked every luxurious idea from the ancients and enriched their own modern pleasures with the tradition of ancient luxury'.

Dashwood created the Hellfire Caves out of existing chalk mines at West Wycombe. The caves are entered through an impressive Gothic forecourt, from where a long, winding tunnel leads down to the Banqueting Hall and on across a miniature River Styx to the inner temple at the heart of the hill. The Dashwood Hellfire Club met here for their orgiastic masquerades and banquets, well on the way down the slippery slope towards the hellfire that the pious felt they were destined for.

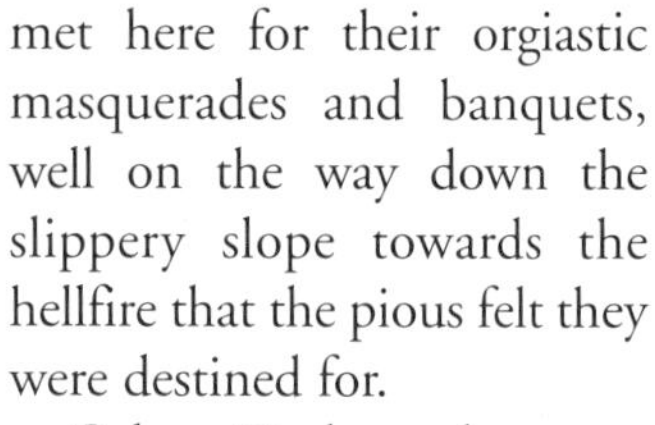

Other Dashwood attractions on site include a vast hexagonal, roofless Dashwood mausoleum of 1765 and the hilltop Church of St Lawrence with its crowning golden globe.

CHEESE ROLL

Stilton, Cambridgeshire

They may roll cheeses down steep hills in Gloucestershire (see page 97), but the famous Stilton cheese is celebrated entirely on the level during the annual May Day celebrations at Stilton village.

Cheese-rolling at Stilton is one of those fascinating customs that you would expect to have come rolling

LEFT: *A rather decorous representation of Hellfire Club cavorting at the Hellfire Caves. It was much more fun in the flesh...*

out of the mists of time. But cheese-rolling seems to have been the mid-20th century creation of an inspired pub landlord, keen to promote the village on the tourist trail. It worked a treat.

Stilton cheese enjoys a rich, ripe and reeking pedigree as it is. It's said to have its origins in an original home-made cheese that was sold by the landlord of a Stilton pub during the 18th century, although Stilton is not made in the village today, but in various dairies throughout Leicestershire, Nottinghamshire and Derbyshire. There is a strict designation of origin, as with sherry and champagne.

The village has a colourful May Day festival anyway, but the highlight of the day is definitely the afternoon cheese-rolling, during which about 20 teams of four race and roll cheeses along a 45-metre (147-foot) course for the coveted title of Stilton Cheese Rolling Champion of Champions. Some teams are in fancy dress and the mood of the event is unfailingly fun-filled and full of spirits, in more ways than one. Prizes are a whole Stilton cheese, and bottles of port. Have they ever had a team on stilts? That's the question.

ABOVE: *The magnificent and regal swan manages to conflate elegance and grace with a very bizarre face. Counting swans en masse must make for a nightmare.*

Swanning Around on the Swashes

Ouse Washes, Cambridgeshire

Calling all Ugly Ducklings – you *will* grow up to be beautiful, if the annual Festival of Swans on the wetlands of the Ouse Washes that straddle the Cambridgeshire and Norfolk border is anything to go by in terms of the seemingly flawless grace of swans en masse. The two-day festival takes place in late November and celebrates the arrival of the wintering flocks. There are tours, events, lectures, an artist-in-residence, and, of course, plenty of swans.

The swan is Britain's largest and most graceful bird, elegant, effortless in its waterborne glide, yet weighing in at 9 kilograms (10 pounds). Landing swans are the Concordes of the water world. Long known as 'royal' birds, swans formerly belonged to the Crown, and only people with a special licence from the Monarch were allowed to keep them. On the Thames they are still owned by the Queen, and the Vintners' and Dyers' companies, and the practice of 'swan-upping' – when they are rounded up and marked with nicks on their beaks – ensures that the owner can be identified.

The dramatic wetlands on the Ouse Washes are home to some of the most spectacular winter gatherings of wild swans. Swans are not the only birds present, of course, and the wetlands offer fine bird-watching all year round.

In the past swans were prized as a delicacy at upper-crust banquets and came close to being seriously reduced in numbers. They are now protected by law. You're well-advised not to get too close, anyway, especially to a nesting swan. One blow from those powerful wings alone can break bones, and those great beaks, backed by rather menacing eyes, can deliver a bit of a bash. Fortunately, with 20,000 swans now thriving in Britain, there's little chance of a swan's swan song nowadays.

Bearing The Brunt

Whittlesey, Cambridgeshire

The last wild bear in Britain was killed centuries ago, but a bear of sorts still dances through the streets of Whittlesey each January at the annual Straw

LEFT: ***The Triangular Lodge at Rushton, where Sir Thomas Tresham's triangular take triumphed totally.***

Bear Festival. This is one of England's most ancient and fascinating traditions, the precise origins of which are a mystery. The event originally took place on Plough Monday – the first Monday after Twelfth Night and the day when farm workers went back to work after the Christmas festivities.

In other towns and villages a mock plough known as a Fool Plough would be dragged through the streets while the ploughmen solicited donations of food, money and beer from the residents for one final booze-up before work began. In Whittlesey, however, rather than a plough, a ploughman or farm lad was dressed up as a Straw Bear. Lengths of tightly twisted straw were tied round his arms, legs and body, while a straw cone – the bear's head – sat on his shoulders. Hardly able to see, the Bear was hauled around from door to door and put through a mock dance until the householder made a donation.

The Straw Bear Festival declined during the late 19th century, and ceased to be run from 1909 onwards when local police officially banned the event as being a 'public nuisance'. The custom was revived in 1980, and for the first time in 70 years a Straw Bear appeared in the streets of Whittlesey and danced its way from pub to pub accompanied by a merry throng of musicians, dancers and spectators. It is now an annual event, with over 250 performers and musicians gathering in the town for a week of festivities.

The Bear dances on the Saturday before Plough Monday and on Sunday the straw costume is ceremonially burned.

Three-cornered Token of the Trinity

Rushton, Northamptonshire

Sir Thomas Tresham had no great love for all things square, but took to triangles in a big way. The problem was, he had spent too many years languishing in square prison cells because of his determined devotion to the Roman Catholic faith. This was not a rewarding allegiance in the anti-Catholic England of the late 16th century, but Sir T was nothing if not determined. In the course of things he developed an obsession with triangular symbolism.

During his time in prison Sir Thomas mulled over ways of enshrining his beliefs, and his defiance, and came up with the idea of creating a unique building that would reflect his fixation with the concept of the Holy Trinity. On his release in 1593 he set about building the Triangular Lodge.

The lodge is in the shape of an equilateral triangle, with each side 33 feet 3 inches (10.18 metres for spoilsports) long, and the Trinity theme is repeated throughout the building – three floors, three triangular roof gables, and three triangular windows on each floor. There are even inscriptions along the edge of the upper walls, all with 33 letters. Almost everything about the building, apart from the stones from which

ABOVE: *A Conkering Conquistador takes aim at a horny old chestnut during the World Conker Championships at Ashton.*

it is made, relates to the number three. Sir T could hardly get by with triangular bricks.

In spite of its truly remarkable exterior, the Triangular Lodge is rather plain inside, and Sir Thomas never lived here himself. It became home to the estate's warrener who, hopefully, caught more than three rabbits in his life.

More Than One Way to Crack a Nut

Ashton, Northamptonshire

Cracking conkers may be seen as a traditional pastime for schoolkids, but in the village of Ashton by the River Nene, near Oundle, they take the game of conkers very seriously. It's here, outside the Chequered Skipper pub, that the annual World Conker Championships is staged on the second weekend in October each year.

Conkers are the hard, shiny fruit of the horse chestnut tree, a species introduced from the Balkans in the 16th century. The playground sport of threading a chestnut onto a length of cord and then bashing an opponent's chestnut by striking it with your own is said to have first been recorded in the 1840s on the Isle of Wight.

The World Conker Championships was founded in Ashton in the early 1960s when a group of local pub-goers found their usual hobby of fishing rained off by the wet autumn weather. Ashton village has plenty of fine horse chestnut trees, so a game of conkers was an obvious wet-weather diversion, with the loser buying the beer.

From this the World Championships grew. Today a couple of hundred people take part and spectators run into the thousands. Money raised goes to the Royal National Institute for the Blind and the event is presided over by the reigning King Conker, who wears one string of conkers to mark each year of victory. Some champs even wear conker-covered shoes and caps.

Conkers may seem a very simple game, but aficionados relish the subtle nuances of technique and style. There are now pages of rules and regulations, and stewards and umpires oversee every match. All conkers used in the competitions are provided by the Ashton Conker Club, thus avoiding such subtle refinements as soaking the conkers in vinegar or linseed oil.

Entries for the championship are truly worldwide, but the British retain dominance, although few care to reminisce about 1976, when the title was taken by a Conkering Conquistador from Mexico.

Gloucestershire, Warwickshire, Herefordshire & Worcestershire

The serene counties of the English and Welsh borderlands have an irresistible charm that springs from their deep-seated rural character and palpable sense of history. For many years the region now covered by Gloucestershire, Warwickshire, Herefordshire and Worcestershire lay along the fault-line of conflict between Celtic Wales and the England of the Romans, Anglo Saxons and Normans. This is a region of historic towns and villages, of landscapes beautified by the shapely hills of the Cotswolds and by some of England's finest surviving woodland. Scattered throughout are a number of remarkable buildings that include exotic mansions, medieval dovecotes, and an Italianate church, while the tradition of eccentric festivals is alive and well in the form of breakneck cheese-rolling, batty ball games and the subtle art of shin kicking.

Domes & Dovecotes, Chained Chapters & Chucking Cheeses

JENNER THE JAB

Berkeley, Gloucestershire

You can thank an eccentric, but hugely talented, 18th-century doctor for all the immunization jabs you endured as a child, or before you set off on an exotic holiday.

Edward Jenner, the 'father' of vaccination, was born in Berkeley in 1749, and trained in London. He came home to Gloucestershire to practise medicine, his profession for 50 years. Among many interests, Jenner was a dedicated naturalist, famed for his knowledge of the nesting habits of the cuckoo. He also studied geology, and discovered a fine Plesiosaur skeleton. More daringly, Jenner experimented with flying. He even built and flew a hydrogen balloon only one year after the Montgolfier brothers completed their first hot air balloon flight.

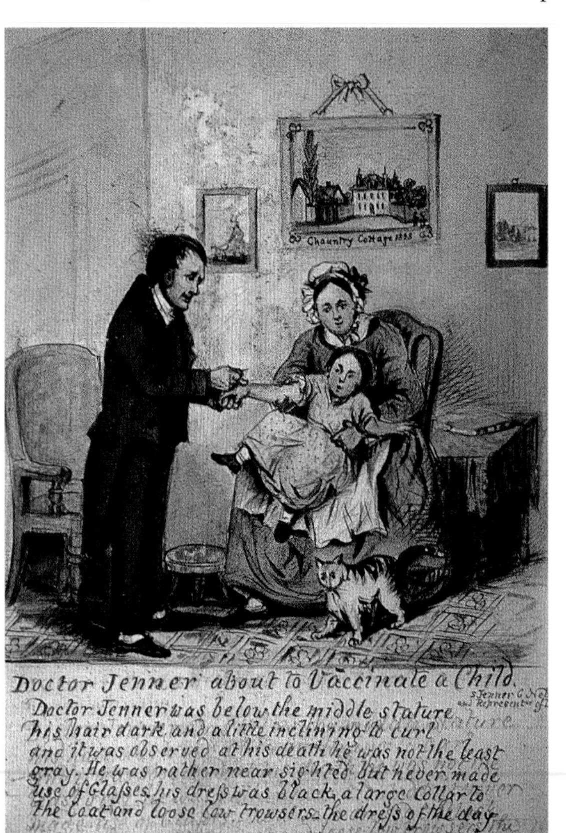

Apart from such fruitful and odd activities, Jenner is best remembered for his breakthrough work on vaccination. In Jenner's day smallpox inoculation was well-established, but it had serious disadvantages: until the infection subsided, the inoculated patient had smallpox and could infect others.

As a country doctor Jenner was well aware of the enduring image of the rosy-cheeked milkmaid, an image sustained by the fact that milkmaids who had suffered from the relatively harmless cowpox disease never seemed to catch the related and often deadly smallpox. Not only did they avoid a killer disease, their complexions remained rosy and unravaged.

Jenner reasoned that exposure to cowpox had made them immune to smallpox, and in 1796 put the theory to the test by infecting an eight-year-old farm boy, James Phipps, with cowpox. He then infected the boy with smallpox and little James proved to be immune. Jenner had made the breakthrough, although the ethics of the case are questionable from our modern perspective. At the time his activities were attacked fiercely by some fellow physicians, yet his work boosted the science of immunology. In 1979 smallpox was finally declared eradicated.

Queen Anne House in Berkeley was Jenner's home and surgery, and it is now the Jenner Museum. There is a re-creation of his study, together with displays about immunology, and in the garden is the Temple of Vaccinia, or Cowpox Temple, a rustic summerhouse where Jenner used to treat the local poor against the pox.

Yew And The Devil

Painswick, Gloucestershire

The well-kept churchyard of St Mary's Church in the beautiful Cotswold village of Painswick may be a tranquil spot, but it's the Devil who does the gardening.

The churchyard is planted with ancient yew trees, and this is where the Devil comes in. There are exactly 99 trees. The number has always been the same and locals will tell you that this is because the Devil favours the number 99. Every time a 100th tree has been introduced it withers and dies.

Devilish things certainly happened to Painswick during the English Civil War. At one time, in 1644, the church was occupied by Parliamentarian forces and when Royalists attacked the village, St Mary's was damaged. The church's outer walls are still pockmarked with bullet and cannon holes.

St Mary's is much loved and protected these days. Every September the Painswick Clypping ceremony takes place in the churchyard. The term has nothing to do with trimming the yews – leave that to Old Nick – but comes from the Saxon word *ycleping* , meaning 'embracing'. On the day, locals join hands and encircle the church in an act of dedication.

Such devotion works, if the charm of St Mary's is anything to go by, although the churchyard is probably best avoided during storms – the church has twice been struck by lightning. In 1765 a thunderbolt dislodged a few stones from the tower and caused the bells to ring, and in 1883 another strike knocked down the top 9 metres of the spire. Perhaps someone was trying to plant that 100th yew...

ABOVE: ***Clypping the Church of St. Mary's at Painswick without a devious devil in sight.***

OPPOSITE: ***Jenner the Jab as seen by the media of the day. There seemed more interest in his lush locks and orderly dress than in his anonymous pincushion patient.***

PREVIOUS PAGE: ***The stuff of nightmare at Snowshill manor. This magnificent samurai armour strikes a splendidly bizarre note in deepest Gloucestershire.***

Rock & Rolling Cheese

Brockworth, Gloucestershire

Hard cheese is the order of the day on May Bank Holiday at Cooper's Hill, Brockworth, when scores of high risk eccentrics hurtle down a steep hillside, racing in pursuit of a Double Gloucester cheese. The cheese measures 30 centimetres (around 1 foot) in diameter and weighs nearly 4 kilograms (8 pounds), and there are four races. Each one starts when a cheese is launched downhill and the runners take off in manic trajectories. This is no casual downhill lope. The hill in question is extremely steep; you would need to sidle sideways in a series of very tight zig-zags just to walk down safely.

Unfortunately, when properly aimed downhill a big round cheese follows a straight but bouncing line, with

'I'VE GOT OTHER STUPID THINGS TO DO.'

Cheese-rolling competitor with broken ankle

the result that few of the cheese-chasers remain on their feet for long. They either end up pitching cheese-over-chin, or more sensibly they curl up and roll. The first 'runner' to reach the bottom of the hill grabs the recumbent cheese and takes it home, along with cuts, bruises and an occasional broken limb.

The event has long been controversial because of the high number of injuries that results. In 1997 at Cooper's Hill there were 18 serious injuries and the race winner, local postman Craig Carter, broke his arm, though he still seemed content. It was a fair match; he had broken the other arm when he won in 1994. Also in 1997, a neck-craning bystander was hit on the head by the hurtling cheese. He was knocked down and skidded to the bottom of the hill, bruised, battered and straight into a waiting ambulance.

How did it all begin? One theory is that cheese-rolling is similar to ancient wheel burning ceremonies that are still enacted worldwide to celebrate the arrival of summer. The burning wheel is said to represent the horizon-rolling sun, a genuine 'big cheese'.

The Cooper's Hill devotees see nothing eccentric about their 'sport' and they even stage secondary cheese rolling competitions at lesser venues in the area.

The big question remains; does a downhill roll improve the taste of a cheese roll?

A TOUCH OF THE ORIENT

Sezincote, Gloucestershire

The sensational Sezincote House, with its huge, copper-clad, onion-shaped dome and its minarets, looks more like a Mughal mosque than a Georgian country pile. It's a triumph of imagination over manners.

The Sezincote estate was bought by Colonel Sir Charles Cockerell when he returned from many years of service with the British East India Company in Bengal in the early years of the 19th century. Fired by memories of exotic buildings and life styles, Sir Charles set about recreating a building that was recognizably Indian. His brother, Samuel Pepys Cockerell, played a great part in the work.

The exterior of Sezincote celebrates the classic features of North Indian Islamic architecture, and while the interior is Greek Revival, the master bedroom contains a four-poster bed that incorporates the Colonel's Bengal tent poles, and is topped with another Mughal dome. The future George IV, as Prince Regent at the time, is said to have visited Sezincote and to have taken the building as inspiration for the Royal Pavilion, Brighton (see page 56).

Sezincote is a marvellous mix of Indian styles and is a rare reflection of the early days of the British Empire in India when a celebration of native style and culture was enthusiastically embraced and celebrated before the emergence of the snobbery and aloofness that characterized the later heyday of the Raj.

The gardens at Sezincote were also inspired by Sir Charles's Eastern experiences. They are dotted with statues and with temples to Hindu Gods, and the Oriental water gardens are complete with an Oriental bridge that is flanked by statues of Nandi the Bull, Shiva's mount.

Sezincote's gardens were restored with great skill in the 1960s and can be visited from January to November on Thursdays and Fridays and Bank Holiday Mondays.

COLLECTOR'S PARADISE

Broadway, Gloucestershire

Unlike sensational Sezincote, Snowshill Manor is a traditional house, English to the bones of its good

Cotswold stone; but behind the solid façade there lurks an exceptionally eccentric exhibition of artefacts.

We all collect things, and cannot let go. But Charles Paget Wade took collecting to new levels of obsessiveness; thankfully so, for the rest of us. Wade's family motto was *Nequid pereat*, 'Let nothing perish', and he clung to that dictum tenaciously. Snowshill contains many of the finest collections of arts and crafts in Britain. Ceramics and glassware, dolls and doll's houses, miniatures and rare books, clocks, toys, model train sets, and bicycles are only a few of the items on display. The house became so full that Charles Wade decamped to a cottage in the grounds.

ABOVE: ***The Samurai at Snowshill Manor where collect-o-mania is celebrated in spectacular fashion.***

Above the door to the music room is the inscription 'Man is carried to heaven on the wings of music'. Inside, brass, percussion, woodwind and string instruments are arranged in the form of a small orchestra. Other items include quirkier instruments such as serpent horns and hurdy-gurdies, together with statues and paintings, tapestries and lace work. The famous Green Room contains the armoury, which includes 26 suits of Japanese samurai armour, carefully set out to create a fabulous tableau.

ABOVE: ***Snowshill Manor's eccentric collector's paradise is all under cover at this otherwise typical English idyll of mossy stonework and leafy trees.***

Snowshill is in the care of the National Trust and can be visited Wednesday to Sunday from Easter to October and on Mondays in July and August.

Alternative Olympicks

Dover's Hill, Gloucestershire

Forget the stunning displays of athleticism at the Olympic Games – an equally thrilling alternative takes place each year at Dover's Hill, near Chipping Camden, when Robert Dover's Cotswold Olympicks get under way.

Dover's Olympicks include the delightfully esoteric sports of shin-kicking and cudgel and slingstick, all established in 1612 by Robert Dover, a Cambridge-educated lawyer. Dover was an extrovert and genial eccentric who infused the games with terrific panache. The original games included a mock Dover's Castle, complete with firing cannon, with Dover directing activities from horseback, wearing a ruff and feathered hat, plus hare coursing, horse races, foot races, wrestling, and fencing with staffs. Card games and chess competitions also played their part. The games were hugely popular and even Shakespeare is believed to have attended, near the end of his life.

Dover's Olympicks were suspended when the Civil War began but were in full swing again by the early 18th century. As with so many old time traditions, however, the games drew wearisome complaints from Victorian England's moral crusaders and were finally ended in 1852, because of alleged 'rowdiness'.

Dover's Hill is now in the care of the National Trust. The games were revived in the 1950s and have continued annually ever since. Spectators can watch all manner of sports not seen at the real Olympics – a wheelbarrow marathon, tug of war, sack racing, and of course the noble game of shin-kicking. This is a game for two. Contestants stand face to face, grip each other by the shoulder and by the belt, and then try to up-end each other by vigorous shin-kicking. The game is thought to have originated as part of an early form of wrestling, and a couple of hundred years ago experts wore iron-tipped boots and trained for matches by beating their own shins with a hammer. The modern version permits the wearing of shin pads. Today's Premier League footballers are tap dancers by comparison.

Dover's Olympicks take place annually at the end of May and are followed on the day after by the processions and festivities of the longstanding Scuttlebrook Wake.

On the Ball in Atherstone

Atherstone, Warwickshire

Football may be England's most popular sport, but in the old market town of Atherstone they play a very different kind of ball game.

The Atherstone Ball Game has been played through the streets of this old market town every Shrove Tuesday since medieval times. It resembles similar events that are celebrated in other locations, including Sedgefield in County Durham, and St Ives and St Columb Major in Cornwall. Many other villages probably had similar events, now long forgotten.

The origins of these traditional events are uncertain, but one gruesome suggestion is that they derive from ancient battles, at which the severed heads of enemies were kicked about the battlefield. In Cornwall the ball game is known as 'hurling', an ancient sport that had well-defined rules, involving rival parishes competing to deliver the ball across their own boundary. These were deadly serious confrontations and 16th-century records mention players suffering 'bloody pates, bones broken and out of joint'.

The ball used at Atherton is about 38 centimetres (15 inches) in diameter and is made of leather. The game is launched when the ball is thrown from an upstairs window of a town bank into the eager crowd. After that it's mayhem as people struggle to get a touch of the ball or to claim one of the ribbons that are tied to it. Whoever is in possession of the ball two hours later is the winner.

Atherton's Ball Game is said to have been played at one time by teams from rival counties Warwickshire and Leicestershire. The prize was a bag of gold and the right to serve in the army for a year – a guarantee of a regular wage. Today, just taking part is reward enough and there is great kudos in being the person in possession of the ball when the game ends. There's no mention of yellow cards. And they board up the shop windows.

ABOVE: ***Unchain your brain at Hereford Cathedral's famous Chained Library, where numerous rare volumes are kept securely in situ by a system of chains.***

CHAINED CHAPTERS

Hereford, Herefordshire

Forget library cards, body scanners and the book amnesties of modern libraries, medieval churches chained their precious tomes to the wall in a bid to thwart overly possessive readers.

Hereford Cathedral has the finest such library in the world. The cathedral's theological books, often many volumes long, were precious and unique, having been written by hand in elaborate calligraphy, and they were kept secure by a system of chains and rods. One end of a chain would be attached to the decorated leather cover of a book, with the other locked onto a metal rod running along the base of each shelf. The chain was long enough for the book to be taken down and read at a desk, but no thieving bibliophile could slip the volume under their coat and do a runner. The books were shelved with their spines facing inwards so that there was no need to turn them round when they were taken down, thus avoiding tangling the chain.

There has been a theological library at Hereford Cathedral since the 12th century, though the current chained bookcases date from the 17th century. It is the largest surviving chained library in the world. Amongst the 1500 chained books there are 229 medieval manuscripts, including the 8th-century Hereford Gospels.

The chained books can be seen in their original arrangement in a specially designed chamber; but there's no way you can borrow any of these volumes for holiday reading.

BELLISSIMO TOWER

Hoarwithy, Herefordshire

Deep at the heart of a very English landscape, at Hoarwithy above the River Wye, stands a very Italian church complete with tall campanile and cloistered arcade. It dates from the latter part of the 19th century and was described by Nikolaus Pevsner, masterful chronicler of English architecture, as being 'South Italian Romanesque and semi-Byzantine'.

Hoarwithy's St Catherine's Church was the life's work, to the point of obsessiveness, of the Reverend William Poole – a man of substantial independent means who spent nearly 50 years lavishing attention on the creation of an Italianate church. It replaced an existing modest building that still survives, unseen, as part of the Italianate successor. Poole even brought in craftsmen from Italy to add the authentic touch. Several married locally and their descendants still live in the district.

BELOW: ***The terrific Italianate campanile of Hoarwithy's Church of St Catherine fits neatly into an English pastoral scene.***

St Catherine's has a fine hilltop position, an ideal site for showing off its campanile, the distinctive Italian-style bell tower with pierced lights and pyramidal top that soars skywards, partly framed by tall trees.

Rev. Poole did not stint on the interior of the church either. The marble columns of the chancel support a dome and there is a golden apse to the east displaying a mosaic of Christ as Ruler of the World. Much use was made of white and green marble, porphyry, and lapis lazuli; multi-coloured slabs cover the floors. Sturdy oak choir stalls recapture a more English feel, but the overall impression is still engagingly sunny south in style.

A Broad View From Broadway

Broadway, Worcestershire

One of England's finest follies, Broadway Tower, was built on the whim of a grande dame, who glanced out of her window and swore that she could see a distant hilltop.

The *dame* in question was Lady Coventry who was convinced that she could see the top of the 312-metre (1023-foot) Fish Hill from her house in Worcester 30 kilometres away. Lady Coventry ordered a beacon to be lit on top of the hill and could easily see its glow. Having proved her point she then persuaded her wealthy husband to build the folly as a mock castle tower.

Today, the tower adds a fine flourish to the summit of Fish Hill above the beautiful village of Broadway. It offers panoramic views of 12, 13, or 14 counties, depending on which enthusiast you listen to; but there's a stunning outlook, regardless of the finer details, and on a clear day you can see forever – or at least to mountainous Wales.

Broadway Tower was once lived in by William Morris, doyen of the late 19th -century Arts & Crafts Movement. It was the perfect retreat for the group of painters known as the Pre-Raphaelites, who revelled in the medieval ambience and the exhilarating views.

Broadway Tower is a focal point of an attractive country park and can be visited. There are also exhibitions about the country park and the Pre Raphaelites. And all because the Lady had a view.

Buckets of Dovecotes

Hawford and Wichenford, Worcestershire

Pigeon-racing is a hugely popular pastime today; but at one time keeping pigeons was the preserve of the wealthy. They bred them for food rather than fancy.

The special buildings in which pigeons roosted were called dovecotes and were once an essential feature of great estates and manor farms. During the medieval period there were probably about 30,000 dovecotes scattered throughout Britain. Some were big enough to house over 1000 birds and most were freestanding in open country, which may account for the eccentric custom of making them highly decorative, so that they stood out as something beyond their function. Several fine examples survive.

Pigeons were a useful and often essential source of food at a time when livestock had to be killed at the onset of winter. Their use was partial, however. Humble farmers were usually banned from keeping dovecotes, but monasteries and the lord of the manor owned palatial specimens. The fact that the plumptious birds were fattening themselves on the corn of a poor farmer was of no account in such inequitable days.

Doves and pigeons also provided guano, from which saltpetre – a component of gunpowder – could be extracted. Feathers were used for bedding and tanners used the manure to treat leather.

Today you can visit a couple of timber-framed late medieval dovecotes that are now in the care of the National Trust. One is at Hawford and was part of a monastery. The other is at Wichenford and dates from the 17th century.

Picking The Locks

Tardebigge, Worcestershire

Canals are nothing if not direct, and when it comes to climbing, they often surmount hefty hills that get in the way. Britain's canal builders of the Industrial Age were remarkable engineers who could literally move mountains. On the Worcester and Birmingham Canal they installed 58 locks to ascend 130 metres (426 feet) between the River Severn and Birmingham. At Tardebigge, between Redditch and Bromsgrove, 30 of these locks leap 66 metres (216 feet), the longest flight of locks in the country.

The Tardebigge Locks were opened in 1815 after an original plan for boat lifts had been abandoned because it was felt that supplying regular power to them was not possible. A lift had been in operation until 1815, however and was a remarkable engineering feature in its own right. It could raise 64 tonnes and required only two men to wind it manually. This either reflected exceptional engineering, or exceptional men. The lift dock was later incorporated into the lock system.

Tardebigge Locks are operational today for leisure use by narrow -boats. They are a remarkable feature within the landscape and remain as a token of an outstanding age of engineering that saw its way determinedly through the straight and narrow.

BELOW: ***Canal locks as far as the eye can see at Tardebigge, where 30 locks rise through 66 metres (216 feet).***

Shropshire, Staffordshire, Derbyshire, Nottinghamshire & Lincolnshire

Strapped across the waist of England, between Wales and The Wash is a chain of counties whose names resonate with British character. Shropshire, Staffordshire, Derbyshire, Nottinghamshire and Lincolnshire represent a large swathe of the country. They embrace a variety of landscapes, from the rich pastoral countryside of Shropshire and Staffordshire to the exhilarating moors of Derbyshire's Peak District and the flat wetlands of the Lincolnshire Fens. There is a huge variety of eccentric places and activities too. Here you will find the world's first iron bridge and an ancient castle tower that out-leans the Leaning Tower of Pisa, as well as astonishing festivals and events that include a gang of Boggans, horned dancers, Plague Sunday, and the world toe-wrestling championship.

Twisting Toes & Twistly Towers, Horns, Hoods & A House of Straws

HUNGOVER CASTLE

Bridgnorth, Shropshire

Forget the Leaning Tower of Pisa, you'll get a crick in the neck if you spend too much time staring at the Leaning Tower of Bridgnorth.

This remarkable 20-metre (65-foot) high tower at the heart of the Shropshire countryside leans at an angle of 15 degrees, three times the angle of Pisa's famous landmark. It's Oliver Cromwell's fault. He and his Civil War gunners left Bridgnorth Castle wrecked after a siege in 1646.

In typical ruthless fashion, Cromwell had the castle blown up. The great square-cut keep toppled so far, but no further, and there it stayed while the ruins of the rest of the castle slowly decayed or were plundered for stone over the years. Today, the Leaning Tower is a central feature of a public park, and it really does turn your head.

The original castle was built on a promontory commanding the River Severn and the surrounding countryside. It dates from 1101 and was founded by Robert de Belleme, who subsequently became Earl of Shrewsbury. De Belleme seems to have been the Anglo-Norman precursor of the infamous Vlad the Impaler, the 15th-century Romanian model for Bram Stoker's

RIGHT: *Ultimate ironwork at the Iron Bridge on the River Severn. The challenge of building the bridge has been compared to that of building a glass bridge today.*

PREVIOUS PAGE: *Everything neatly in place at Mr Straw's House in Worksop, where the world was frozen in time during the 1930s.*

Dracula. Vlad was so named because of his custom of skewering locals who displeased him. De Belleme is said to have used meat hooks to impale victims of his displeasure. He was a kidnapper and murderer, often starving his victims to death, and was said to have torn out the eyes of his godson in a fit of pique. Eventually the scheming earl plotted against Henry I, who promptly captured Bridgnorth Castle and imprisoned de Belleme for life.

Bridgnorth's Leaning Tower has survived all of this, while Bridgnorth itself is a delightful place. It is in two parts, High Town and Low Town, the two separated by a sandstone cliff that is negotiated by flights of steps and by a remarkable cliff railway that opened in 1892. It's 66 metres (216 feet) long and has a vertical rise of 37 metres (121 feet), a gradient of 1 in 1.5.

Heavy Metal

Ironbridge, Shropshire

You can't burn bridges at Coalbrookdale on the River Severn, where the world's first cast-iron bridge still spans the gliding stream. Yet Coalbrookdale's famous 18th-century bridge was built using the techniques of carpentry. The importance of the iron bridge cannot be exaggerated. Considered totally eccentric at the time, it became the template for a flourish of iron buildings from London's Paddington Station to the famous Crystal Palace. Thousands flocked to see the bridge, among them, poets, painters and even early industrial spies.

The builders of the bridge were unsentimental creatures. They gave their innovative structure no

ringing title other than Iron Bridge – a name that soon transferred itself to the entire area. This was the era of red-hot industrialization in Britain; Shropshire and the River Severn were at the heart of it all.

Ironworks and potteries had flourished in the Coalbrookdale area for many years and by the 1770s, a bridge across the Severn had become essential. It was decided to use iron, although the use of iron in major structures had not been tried. The bridge was a substantial challenge; it was 60 metres (196 feet) long; the main span was 30 metres (98 feet) wide; and the bridge stood 14 metres (46 feet) above the Severn.

ABOVE: ***The Flushed With Pride galleries at the Gladstone Pottery Museum confront, with cheerful panache, the behind-the-scenes world of sanitation.***

What makes the iron bridge remarkable is that it was built using wood-working techniques. Most of the joints between the various parts were traditional carpentry devices such as mortice and tenon joints and dovetails. The bridge was coated with pitch to protect it from rusting. Most modern engineers would lament the lack of quality control that accompanied the construction of the iron bridge, but most are in awe of its innovative status. A vivid comparison suggests that it was the equivalent of trying to build a glass bridge today.

By the early 20th century the bridge still functioned, although an inward movement of the riverbanks was distorting its frame. In the 1980s large concrete bulwarks were sunk into the riverbed in an effort to halt this. Today the Coalbrookdale area is designated as a World Heritage Site. As well as the famous iron bridge there are several fascinating museums in the area.

Flushed And Fascinated

Stoke-on-Trent, Staffordshire

The remarkable Flushed With Pride exhibition galleries within the Gladstone Pottery Museum in Longton, Stoke-on-Trent, cast a charming light on a subject that most of us would much rather leave behind.

The Gladstone Museum is a fascinating place overall; it's the only complete Victorian pottery factory in existence and is a unique working museum that tells the vivid story of England's 19th-century pottery industry. A major part of that industry was linked to sanitation and the museum's Flushed with Pride section tells the story with panache.

The loo is the great leveller, the unavoidable void, the unglamorous gulf, the triumph of function over our fantasy lives of smooth, svelte glamour; but the Flushed exhibition brings fascination to the equation. Here you can pore over the history of sanitation from prehistoric squat, to the launch of the water closet and the potential 'greening' of future loos.

The museum is cleverly curated and manages to bring enthusiasm and entertainment to the world of loo-tech through a series of displays that take you into the cloacal world of sewers, to the odours, echoes and effulgences of everyday loo-life, that is entertaining as well as informative; although the section promising a 'hands-on interactive gallery' might give you pause.

There's excellent insight into the technology and engineering of sanitation and its contribution to good health. It's a sobering insight for those of us who take effortless sanitation for granted and a timely reminder of how many parts of the world lack even the most basic facilities. Other quirky items focus on how astronauts and others in extreme situations handle their needs. One absolute certainty is that loos have a future and there is an intriguing section that looks at future sanitation and the potential for compost toilets and small-scale treatment plants

A Clean & Decent section eases you smoothly into the far more glamorous world of toilet décor with

ABOVE: ***Dancing with Deer; the Abbots Bromley deer dancers in fine form as they celebrate one of England's most fascinating traditions.***

displays of decorated wash stands, antique baths and an 'avocado bathroom suite' – the archetypal theme of a myriad suburban loos.

The Gladstone Pottery Museum is open daily, all year.

Horns In Plenty

Abbots Bromley, Staffordshire

At Abbots Bromley on the 26th August, you may bump into a group of men prancing about with stags' antlers on their shoulders. Say nothing; just accept that there's a point to it all and enjoy one of England's most revered traditions.

There are written records of the Horn Dance having been performed as early as the 13th century. Three sets of carved wooden 'heads' in colours of red, white and blue are used; they are said to be 16th century in design and attached to them are real stags' horns. The largest pair weighs 11.5 kilograms (25 pounds) and has a span of nearly 1 metre (3 feet).

One of the antlers has been carbon dated to the 11th century and archaeologists have found evidence of antlers that date back to the Neolithic period, over 7000 years ago. They believe that such horns may have been used for ritualistic purposes. The custom of primitive hunters revering and imitating their quarry by donning antlers, wolf skulls and bear heads is well attested. In our fast-food culture, a hamburger on the head doesn't quite match that.

On the morning of the Abbots Bromley Horn Dance the horns are collected from St Nicholas Church at 8 am. The dance group is made up of six Deer-men, a Fool, Hobby Horse, Bowman and Maid Marion. Attendants collect money for the church during the day as the group dance their way through the village and surrounding countryside to the music of a melodeon player. Their route covers an exhausting 16 kilometres (10 miles) and at the end of the day the horns are returned to the church until the following year.

While the Deer-men are off dancing there's lots of fun and games in the village with craft stalls, exhibitions, children's games and plenty of business for the five local pubs. The Deer-men are not the only ones with sore heads the next day.

ABOVE: *Step inside Eyam Hall and discover the strange, heart-rending tale of Eyam's 17th-century plague-stricken villagers and their voluntary isolation.*

TOEREADORS

Wetton, Staffordshire

When the English poke fun at themselves, they do so obliquely by adding plenty of eccentricity, wit and irony. The annual World Toe-wrestling Championship, which takes place at Ye Olde Royal Oak pub in the Peak District village of Wetton every June, is a brilliant example of this.

Toe-wrestling started in 1976 when locals decided to find a sport that the English might stand a chance of winning. The idea seemed a toe-tal winner and the first competitions were held using bar stools as a 'toedium'. The idea is simple: opponents rest their feet on the toedium and lock their big toes together in an inspired parody of arm-wrestling; the aim is to 'toe-down' your opponent's foot.

Inevitably, within a year a Canadian visitor had snatched the championship and that was the end of it, until 1990, when the landlord of Ye Olde Royal Oak discovered a dusty set of rules and got the sport back on to its toes. By 1994 toe-wrestling was a world sport and in 1997 a bid for Olympic Games status was made. It was turned down on the grounds that there was uncertainty over whether it was a summer or winter Olympic discipline. The Frostbite Finals have yet to be held, but perhaps the Canadians might oblige...

RING-A-RING-O'ROSES A POCKET FULL OF POSIES, A-TISHOO! A-TISHOO! WE ALL FALL DOWN

Nursery Rhyme or Plague Song?

RING A RING O' ROSES

Eyam, Derbyshire

The cheerful nursery rhyme 'Ring a ring o'roses' hides a very odd and menacing message behind its innocuous lyrics; and the Derbyshire village of Eyam knows why.

The rhyme is said to refer to the 14th-century pneumonic and bubonic plagues, known as the Black Death, and to the Great Plague of 1665 that killed most of Eyam's people. The rest of the verse goes:

A pocket full of posies,
A-tishoo! A-tishoo!
We all fall down

The posies referred to the custom of carrying sweet-smelling flowers and herbs in the forlorn belief that they were a protection against infection. Sneezing spreads infection, and the innocent-sounding line 'We all fall down' speaks for itself. Nobody got up.

The last bout of bubonic plague in Britain was between 1665 and 1666, when over 100,000 people are said to have died in London alone. Much of the rest of the country escaped the plague, but at Eyam a local tailor received a bundle of old cloth from London that harboured plague-ridden fleas. When infection spread through the village, the far-sighted rector, George Mompesson, discussed the situation with the 350 villagers; they took the courageous decision to remain in isolation in the brave hope of containing the disease.

Food was placed by neighbouring villagers on the outskirts of Eyam, and was paid for with money that was disinfected by being placed in vinegar-filled rock holes. Open-air church services were held at a natural amphitheatre called Cucklet Delph in a bid to reduce infection; but 262 villagers died before the plague ran its course. The rector survived and lived until 1710.

Today Cucklet Delph is the scene of an annual commemorative service that is held on the last Sunday in August. And 'Ring a ring o' roses' echoes harmlessly on...

Screwing Up

Chesterfield, Derbyshire

A twisted church spire is asking for all sorts of twisted tales, and the corkscrewed spire of Chesterfield's parish church has its fair share.

The spectacular twist in the spire of St Mary and All Saints' Church is said to have been caused by the Devil sneezing, or by Lincoln Cathedral's famous imp out on a spree (see page 113). A rather more scandalous myth is that the spire got itself in a twist at the sight of a virgin marriage and that it will only untwist when another such takes place in the church below. Time passes...

Virtuous Chesterfield seems entirely sanguine about this civic slur, possibly because anyone with an ounce of virtue recognizes that the twisted spire can only be the result of distortion of lead cladding on a frame of unseasoned timber.

The spiral statistics are devilish all the same. The spire is 30 metres (98 feet) high and weighs 150 tonnes (165 tons). It is said to sway in high winds and instruments indicate that it corkscrews in alternate directions by a couple of centimetres each year.

RIGHT: ***There's no cork big enough for Chesterfield's famous corkscrew church steeple.***

St Mary's eccentric spire has been twisting in the wind for over 600 years and seems happy to keep things that way for the time being, imps and impropriety apart.

ABOVE AND LEFT: ***Life in Mr Straw's house in a Worksop suburban street was simple, uncluttered and humble yet somehow reassuring.***

A House of Straws

Worksop, Nottinghamshire

In a modest suburban street in the town of Worksop stands a modest suburban house in which nothing has changed for 70 years.

Most of us move with changing times as far as fashion and furnishings go; but there are remarkable eccentrics who simply stop the world in its tracks.

Two such men who took the 'time-capsule' ideal to extremes were Walter and William Straw, who were so devoted to their parents that after the couple's deaths the brothers decided to keep the family home entirely as it was for the rest of their own lives. Their father died in 1932, their mother in 1937, Walter died in 1975, and William lived on until 1990.

After William's death, the Straws' semi-detached house at No 7 Blyth Grove in Worksop was revealed as a startling memorial to the 1930s. Since their mother's death the brothers' Straw had left everything in the house as it was, right down to the newspapers of the day, the canned food in the kitchen, their parents' clothes on hooks and the furniture and the décor of the day. One explanation for their remarkable commitment might be that the devoted Mrs Straw had preserved the house intact after her husband died in 1932. When she died five years later her equally devoted sons continued the custom.

The family owned a grocer's shop which Walter continued to run while brother William abandoned his career as a history teacher at London University and stayed at home. Visitors were not encouraged, although the brothers behaved courteously to all. They never owned a radio, a television, a telephone or any innovative appliance, and, as they grew older, they began to carefully label many of the old furnishings, as if they knew they possessed a remarkable legacy.

After William's death the house came into the care of the National Trust and today it can be visited. The strangeness of Mr Straw's House seems infinitely sad at times, yet it is an astonishing memorial to people who were truly different; eccentric certainly, but also deeply human.

ABOVE: ***Oddly impish; Lincoln Cathedral's famous imp has a distinctly impish look.***

IMPRINT

Lincoln, Lincolnshire

There's nothing like a breath of Beelzebub to give credence to a church or chapel and Lincoln Cathedral has its very own stone imp to add colour to its godly triumph.

The Lincoln Imp is only 30 centimetres (1 foot) high, yet generates a great deal of interest and affection for such a little chap. Lincoln's football team are known as The Imps and the city has adopted the imp as its unofficial symbol.

The imp sits cheerfully at the top of a column in the cathedral's Angel Choir, with one leg across the opposite knee and with a mischievous grin on his impish features. It was probably carved by medieval stonemasons, who often implanted irreligious motifs and accents into the fabric of great churches and cathedrals as a witty comment on good and evil. Gargoyles and grotesques (see page 47) have the same provenance, as do the gambolling angels and everyday scenes of rustic life seen in the tiny tableaux of great cathedrals such as Wells in Somerset (see page 34).

The Lincoln Imp has a classic loopy legend attached to it, of course. Every imp has baggage, and this one is said to have been blown out of hell on a gust of sulphurous wind, only to end up at Lincoln, where he proceeded to wreak havoc in the cathedral until an outraged angel turned him into stone. Some say there were two imps, but one escaped, put a twist in the spire of Chesterfield Church (see page 111) and then fell foul of a witch who turned him into a cat. Who could doubt it?

The Three Ways to Nowhere Bridge

Crowland, Lincolnshire

There's something very forlorn about a bridge with no water beneath it. But when you have three bridges in one and there's not a sign of water anywhere, then things become very odd indeed.

At Crowland in Lincolnshire, however, locals are used to their three-in-one waterless bridge. The bridge was built by the medieval monks of nearby Crowland Abbey to span the three streams of Catwater, Welland, and Nene – names that might well grace a trio of country solicitors.

The monks named the bridge Trinity, a neat fusion of faith and facility, but somewhere along the line the streams disappeared. This was no mean feat, considering that King Edward IV is said to have sailed under Trinity Bridge on his way to Fotheringay Castle. Locals dubbed the bridge The Three Ways To Nowhere. Today the Trinity Bridge shelters a pedestrian walkway used by the good people of Crowland for pleasurable promenading.

A lack of water seems to have been bad news

Boggans 'n the Hood

Haxey, Lincolnshire

Hats, hoods and umbrellas are frequent fliers across the windy flatlands of Lincolnshire, but at the village of Haxey they celebrate the windblown hood of a 14th-century Lady of the Manor with an extremely strange event.

The fascinating Haxey Hood Game is said to have originated when the wife of Sir John de Mowbray was riding near Haxey one Twelfth Night and her black silk hood was whipped away by the wind. No less than 13 eager farm-hands went chasing after it and when the hood was returned to Lady de Mowbray she was so delighted that she donated a slice of land outside Haxey and decreed that the event should be commemorated annually.

Nowadays the Hood Game takes place on 6th January, although preparations begin on Midsummer's day when an official known as The Lord, appoints a Fool and 11 'Boggans' for the next year's event.

There are some splendidly sinister elements about the Hood Game. On the day, the Lord and his Chief Boggan dress in hunting red and wear top hats bedecked with flowers, while the other Boggans wear red tops. The Fool has strips of coloured cloth stitched to his clothes and wears a feathered and beflowered hat. His face is daubed with ochre and soot. They all assemble at the gates of Haxey Church, whereupon the Fool makes an escape bid but is captured and placed on the broken plinth of an old cross, from which he makes a speech explaining the game to the crowd. Damp straw is then lit behind him in a ceremony known as Smoking the Fool. This is said to represent a far darker ritual whereby the Fool was actually smoked over the fire until he gasped for breath. The suggestion that this may represent even more sinister sacrificial events in pagan times hangs in the smoky air.

After the smoking, The Lord and his Boggans, with the Fool in tow, head off to a nearby field where the Hood Game proper begins. This involves muddy scuffles over possession of the Sway Hood – a heavy coil of rope bound in leather that is thrown up in the air at the start of the game. The object is to get the hood to one of four pubs in Haxey and its neighbouring village of Westwoodside. The hood cannot be kicked or thrown and the scrummaging 'sway' of about 200 people tugs and pushes for several glorious muddy hours until one or other pub is reached. Drinking , needless to say, is prodigious.

The origins of this particularly complex tradition seem intermingled with fertility rites, the birth of the New Year and the return of farm workers to the fields after Christmas. The hood may well represent an original head of a sacrificed ox, although competition between an ox head and the silken hood of Lady de Mowbray hardly bears thinking about.

generally for Crowland Abbey. It burned down in AD 930 and again in 1091 and 1146. In 1117 a minor earthquake shook the abbey to its toes and it may have been this earthquake that opened fissures in the earth that began to drain the streams from below Trinity Bridge until no water remained.

During the 18th century a stone effigy was lifted from the ruinous abbey and was placed on Trinity Bridge, where it remains to this day. It is said to be the figure of Christ clutching the world in his hands; but it may simply be a forlorn traveller wondering where on earth – or water – Edward IV's boat has got to.

BELOW AND RIGHT: ***The Trinity Bridge at Crowland keeps your feet dry, whether you walk on top of, or beneath, its arches.***

Cheshire, Lancashire, Yorkshire, Cumbria & Durham

The famous counties that make up the northern regions of England were powerhouses of the Industrial Age that laid the foundations of Britain's prosperity. Too often, however, they bore the brunt of recession and hard times; yet the northern qualities of independence and dry humour have never dimmed and the great northern traditions of inventiveness, enterprise and energy still burn bright. They are richly commemorated in a host of heritage sites, from restored Victorian boat lifts to brilliant art works amid the landscapes of coalfield and steel industry. Old traditions survive also, in odd folk dances, and in events that run the gamut of eccentricity, from coal-carrying races to telling the biggest lies in the world.

Angel & Obelisk, A Palladian Pig Sty & Dracula's Drop-in

UPLIFTING
Northwich, Cheshire

Britain's 19th-century canal-builders were never short of ideas. They built a load of locks at Tardebigge in Worcestershire (see page 103) to link up two canal systems, but when it came to linking the Kent and Mersey Canal with the River Weaver, they were faced with a fairly abrupt 15-metre jump.

If you can't 'lock' them bit by bit, then you lift them, was the answer, and at Northwich, in 1875, the canal-builders installed the first boat lift the world had ever seen, a lift that could hoist two narrow boats at once. The entire structure has been restored and can be visited.

The technology of the boat lift is simple enough; it is the proportions and statistics that are incredible. Two tanks, known as caissons, were installed, Both were 22 metres (72 feet) long, 4 metres (13 feet) wide and 3 metres (10 feet) deep. They weighed 252 tonnes (278 tons) when flooded with water.

The lifts were operated by hydraulics, but by 1908 powerful rams, operated by wheels, pulleys and counterbalances, had been installed.

The boat lift did sterling duty for many years, but

LEFT: *Up she rises! The remarkable boat lift at Northwich was one oddball way of overcoming water's reluctance to float boats uphill.*

PREVIOUS PAGE: *David Kemp's inspired comments on the once great industries of North-east England overlook a recreational footpath through the Consett landscape.*

Carrying Coals to the Maypole

Gawthorpe, Yorkshire

Coal-mining as a major industry may have been swept away by modernization, but in the Yorkshire village of Gawthorpe they still carry bags of coal for a pastime. On Easter Monday each year dedicated competitors take part in the World Coal-carrying Contest – a straightforward, entirely British take on stamina married to eccentricity. The contest involves competitors carting hefty bags of coal along a course of just over 1000 metres (1093 yards). The winner is the quickest 'coil' humper of the day.

The event, as usual, is said to have originated during a good-natured pub argument, in the 1960s, about which of two friends was the fittest. The outcome was a race with a bag of coal on the shoulders and an imaginative local soon realized that out of a quirky one-off a regular event could arise.

Today, the World Coal-carrying Contest is part of Gawthorpe's Maypole celebrations. The coal race starts at the Royal Oak pub, from where contestants set off lugging a 50-kilogram (110-pound) bag of coal towards the celebratory maypole. The world record is just over four minutes and there's a Ladies' record of just over five minutes, for carrying a 25-kilogram sack. Winners get their name in the *Guinness Book of Records.*

Aficionados say that it's the last couple of hundred metres that are the killer and the course soon becomes dotted with dropped sacks and gasping bodies as the contest progresses. They take their pleasures seriously in Yorkshire.

was closed in 1983 because of its deteriorating condition. The entire structure was renovated at the millennium: the renovation work required a mile of welding, 8000 new bolts, and enough paint to cover six football pitches. The result is a fully operational boat lift and a fascinating Heritage site, complete with an operations' centre, displays and exhibitions. You can even take a boat ride in the lift.

Cracking Coconuts

Bacup, Lancashire

On Easter Saturday, in the Lancashire town of Bacup, you'll bump into groups of dancers dressed in black jerseys, striped red-and-white kilts, white stockings and black clogs. On their heads are turban-like hats decorated with coloured feathers and rosettes. Do not adjust your sight. This is just one of England's most fascinating folk dance traditions, the Bacup Nutters Dance.

The event kicks off at the Traveller's Rest pub on the Rochdale to Bacup road. From here, the world-famous Britannia Coconut Dancers set off on a series of dances that take them from boundary to boundary of the town. Music is supplied by the splendid Stacksteads Silver Band

For some dances the dancers wear on their knees, hands and belts, wooden discs known as Nuts, and it is from these that the dance takes its name. The dancers beat the discs in time with the dance music. The final flourish to all this wonderful flummery is that the dancers blacken their faces. You could not squeeze much more eccentricity out of this ensemble.

Five Garland Dances are performed, in which the dancers wear blue and white garlands. The two Nut Dances feature the wearing of the wooden 'nuts'. There are several theories explaining the origins of the Nutters Dance. The most intriguing suggests that the dance was brought to the region by Cornish tin miners who had moved to the coal-mines of Lancashire many years ago. The Cornishmen in their turn are said to have inherited the dances from Algerian or 'Moorish' pirates, who settled in Cornwall and had taken up mining. The similarity of the Nutters dances to Morris dancing, for which some claim a similar 'Moorish' connection, and the blackened faces of the dancers, are claimed as supporting this theory.

Raids on Elizabethan Cornwall by Algerian corsairs are well documented, certainly, but the Lancashire dances may simply be a happy mish-mash of elements of ancient festivals and seasonal celebrations from within Lancashire itself. The blackened faces of the dancers have an obvious connection to the region's coal-mining and it has been suggested that the wooden discs, or nuts, represent knee and hand protectors worn by miners when crawling through narrow passageways.

ABOVE: *Southern England's famous Stonehenge prehistoric site is ably replicated at Ilton in deepest Yorkshire, the work of 19th-century eccentric William Danby.*

YORKHENGE

Ilton, Yorkshire

England's greatest ancient monument, Stonehenge, has a double in distant Yorkshire. The False Stonehenge stands deep at the heart of forestry land near Ilton. It dates from the early 19th century and was the idea of William Danby, a remarkable eccentric and philanthropist who set up an early form of job creation by paying unemployed locals a shilling a day to build a scattering of mock-prehistoric monuments on his land.

Danby also built himself a proper house called New Swinton Hall and took his time over it, adding bits and pieces to the building for over 50 years. He was industrious to the extreme, penning, at the same time, four volumes of his 'Thoughts', all with such exhausting titles as, 'Travelling Thoughts', 'Thoughts Chiefly on Serious Subjects', and 'Thoughts on Various Subjects and Ideas and Realities'. And just when readers thought they'd escaped, up popped 'Extracts from Young's Night Thoughts, with Observations'.

Danby's Stonehenge, or Druid's Temple, as it became known, included the whole gamut of prehistoric monuments, from solitary standing stones and dolmens to the lintel-crowned sarsens of the false Stonehenge. They are all convincing features and resemble other 'false' monuments in other parts of the country, where farmers and locals, with a sense of irony – and large mechanical diggers – build roadside 'prehistoric graves' for visitors to marvel at while missing the real thing several fields away.

Tall tales clung to Danby's Druid's Temple for years. One story tells how Danby offered food and an annuity to anyone who lived as a hermit within the temple for seven years. Several would be hermits took up the challenge, one apparently sticking it out for a number of years before running off screaming. Danby would probably have made the most successful candidate of all.

High Spirits

Swaledale, Yorkshire

You won't get drunk on thin air at Yorkshire's Tan Hill Inn, even though this oddly placed pub is the highest hostelry in England. Tan Hill stands at 536 metres (1758 feet) above sea level, above the lovely Swaledale, one of the most popular of the famous Yorkshire Dales.

The inn is also on the edge of identity when it comes to England's northern counties. It is only a few hundred yards from the border with Cumbria and because of boundary re-organization is technically in County Durham, but officially in Yorkshire. After a few drinks everything becomes crystal clear.

The reason there's a pub in this unlikely location is because several hundred years ago Tan Hill was a busy place: it stood at the junction of several packhorse trails, the motorways of medievalism, and for many years coal was mined in the surrounding hills. Today, Britain's best-known long-distance walking trail, the Pennine Way, passes the inn and, even in midsummer, thirsty walkers as well as car-bound tourists can enjoy open fires along with their drinks.

Tan Hill supplies its own electricity using a generator and is often cosily glowing while power cuts have plunged the winter dales into darkness below. Beer has been known to freeze in the pipes all the same.

ABOVE: ***Finger pointing at Tan Hill Pub high in the hills of the Yorkshire Dales.***

Bridge Over a Troubled Daughter

Glaisdale, Yorkshire

They have great good sense in Yorkshire, but there's sentimentality too, and the handsome Beggar's Bridge over the River Esk at Glaisdale – the beautiful eastern fringe of the Yorkshire Moors – proves the point.

The bridge was built in 1619 by local man Tom Ferris after the death of his beloved wife, Agnes. Tom built the bridge as a memorial to his early courting of Agnes. The young lovers each lived on opposite banks of the river. There was no bridge or handy crossing place in those days, so Tom had to swim across to get to grips with his lady. Agnes's wealthy father refused permission for Tom and Agnes to marry unless Tom made himself a fortune. Tom was the penniless son of a poor sheep farmer so he decided that he would seek his fortune at sea and then come home and marry Agnes. On the night before Tom left, the River Esk was in dangerous spate and the couple could only wave a forlorn goodbye.

In similar stories, one or other of the heartbroken pair usually tries to swim the stream, gets into difficulties, and prompts the other to leap in to help; at which point both are swept off and drowned. Cue in a lachrymose folk ballad that would still be with us. Being a canny Yorkshireman, however, Tom waved goodbye, and then headed off to sea, got involved in routing the Spanish Armada, sailed with Francis Drake to the West Indies, came home with a fortune, and married Agnes. When Agnes died, he built the Beggar's Bridge to prove the point.

Fortune and finance are certainly handled entertainingly in Yorkshire. At nearby Egton village

Palladian Pigsty

Fyling, Yorkshire

Living in a pig sty takes on new meaning in North Yorkshire, where a one-time porkers' pad is now a delightful holiday home.

The pig sty at Fyling, just south of Whitby, has a façade of wooden mock-Doric columns complete with architrave, fluted frieze, pediment and cornice. The creator of this quirky pig-in-a-joke was Squire Barry, who owned the nearby Fyling Hall. He had spent some time Grand Touring through the Mediterranean countries where classical buildings were in great supply. Many of them were no more than picturesque ruins and were used possibly to house farm animals by practical locals. Heritage does not always feed the family.

A popular opera of the time also featured a pig sty with a classical façade, but, whatever the reason, the pigsty as palace graced the Fyling estate for many years. The style of the sty is a bit of a pigsty, because Squire Barry is said to have happily made things up as he went along; but the result is still delightful. The pigs' owners lived in neighbouring cottages, which were more modest exemplars of vernacular Gothic design.

The Fyling Pig sty eventually fell into disuse, but has been skilfully renovated by the Landmark Trust and can be rented as a holiday home with a history. Views to the coast are superb, although the pigs probably did not care.

ABOVE: ***Pigs may or may not fly at Fyling, but this renovated Palladian pigsty is now a delightful holiday home.***

there's a surviving charges board for use of a private toll road in the 1940s. There was a charge of one shilling for a car; but if it was a hearse, the charge was only sixpence. Half-price when you were wholly dead…

ABOVE: *Whitby's ruined abbey still makes a powerful impact on its high hill above the town.* RIGHT: *The interior of Whitby's Church of St Mary has a plethora of quirky furnishings.*

Dracula's Drop-in

Whitby, Yorkshire

High above the Yorkshire port of Whitby stands a ruined abbey and a dark-walled church; together they create one of the most enthralling Gothic backdrops in England. Throw in hugely atmospheric skies and Bram Stoker's famous fictional vampire, Dracula (who leapt ashore in the shape of a black hound from a wrecked ship at Whitby), and you have a film-set to die for.

Whitby is a charming and rewarding town that is wrapped round the seaward channel of the River Esk. From the heart of the old town, the narrow Church Street leads up to a fabulous flight of 199 slate steps that rise steeply to the Church of St Mary and to the ruined abbey.

ABOVE: ***Casting no light on Hoad Hill, where the world's oddest lighthouse, located several kilometres inland, sees no ships and sounds no warnings.***

St Mary's dates from the 11th century, although it has been much altered over the years. The interior is dense with eccentric fittings and furnishings. Eighteenth-century high-sided box pews fill most of the space and are overlooked by galleries and the walls of the church are lined with wooden tablets bearing texts from scripture. Slightly off-centre is a towering pulpit with a big-bellied stove nearby. Fixed to the pulpit are the long stems of huge hearing trumpets said to have been installed so that the partially deaf wife of an incumbent vicar could hear the sermon.

The graveyard of St Mary's is a thicket of slate headstones. Beyond lie the ruins of the abbey, founded in A.D.657 by King Oswy of Northumbria. The abbey had an abbess and housed monks and nuns. In 663 the Synod of Whitby was held here, at which the early Christian Church in England came under the leadership of Rome

The abbey was brutally sacked by Danes in 794, and was finally abandoned in the 16th century at the Dissolution of the Monasteries. The ruins are bleak, but stunning; North Sea winds have eroded the sandstone into strangely blurred forms and the surviving walls soar into the ragged sky. On this high ground the winter winds can be as biting as Dracula's dentures.

A Lighthouse High and Dry

Hoad Hill, Cumbria

Not even the world's worst sailor could bump their boat into Sir John Barrow's lighthouse on Hoad Hill, above the town of Ulverston. The Barrow Memorial Lighthouse is a good 5 kilometres (3 miles) from the sea.

The daft location of the lighthouse is not down to faulty chart-work on the part of the Admiralty; nor is it the result of a dramatic fall in sea level. It's a unique memorial to a man who founded the Royal Geographical Society, was Secretary to the Admiralty and who was a generous patron of numerous famous expeditions.

Sir John Barrow was born in 1764 in Cumbria. He was not a hands-on explorer, but was well-travelled, and was responsible for the funding of many expeditions during the 18th and 19th centuries' heyday of exploration. Journeys that took place with his backing included several trips to find the source of the Niger River, and travels of Sir John Ross, Sir James Clark Ross, and Sir John Franklin to the Arctic and Antarctic. Franklin's ill-fated search for the Northwest Passage was one of Barrow's final projects.

Sir John died in 1848, and the lighthouse was later built on the hill above Ulverston to a design based on the famous Eddystone Lighthouse in the seas off Plymouth.

The Barrow Memorial lighthouse is open during the summer months. You can climb the 112 steps to the Lantern Room, which has never contained a light. There are splendid views over the Lake District, and the sea shines in the distance.

Rusting in Peace

Lindale, Cumbria

John Wilkinson was the original Heavy Metal fan and his cast-iron memorial at Lindale near Grange-over-Sands proves the point. It was touch and go, however, when it came to laying John to rust in the first place. He was buried four times. Iron that one out.

Wilkinson was a key figure of the Industrial Revolution and was known as Iron Mad Wilkinson because of his conviction that iron was the material of the future. He built boats, bridges and pulpits of iron.

Iron Mad was born in Cumbria, and his family ran a furnace in Backbarrow, near Lake Windermere. Young John took to iron like a magnet. In 1748 he built an experimental blast furnace near Wolverhampton and after many failures succeeded in improving the blast process by substituting coal for coke.

Wilkinson played a prominent part in the building of the world's first iron bridge at Coalbrookdale in Shropshire (see page 107) and in 1787 he launched the first iron boat on the River Winster. The event was watched by crowds of mocking sightseers who were certain the boat would sink – like iron. Off it floated and Iron Mad was made. Two years later he patented a method of fashioning spiral grooves to improve the range and accuracy of cannons.

Iron entered Wilkinson's head as well as his soul and he ordered that iron coffins should be kept ready and waiting at his several residences. When he died it was found that the wooden coffin in which his body had been placed was too large to fit inside the iron casket waiting patiently for him. They buried him inside the wooden coffin, in the garden, pending the casting of a larger iron coffin.The new coffin was so large that the grave-diggers could not dig a big enough hole, because they came across solid rock. Iron Mad was again buried in wood, until a larger grave was blasted out of the rock with dynamite. This time John went down into his garden, in his iron coffin beneath his iron obelisk.

Ironically, however, there was no rest for Wilkinson. In 1828 house and garden were sold and, since the new owners were probably not too happy about having someone else's grave in their garden, the great tomb and obelisk were re-sited to a final rusting place at Lindale Church.

> 'MEMBERS OF THE LEGAL PROFESSION AND POLITICIANS ARE BARRED FROM ENTRY.'
>
> ***Rule 7 of the World's Biggest Liar Competition***

ABOVE: ***'Iron Mad' John Wilkinson's iron obelisk at Lindale celebrates a great genius of the Industrial Revolution who was a heavy metal fan to the end of his life.***

Fibbing for Fun

Santon Bridge, Cumbria

The chances of getting an honest answer in the Cumbrian village of Santon Bridge in November are slim. The town is full of talented fibbers, who compete for the title of World's Biggest Liar. The contest has its origins in the remote Lakeland valley of Wasdale,

ABOVE: ***Tax bridging in a big way is said to have been the reason behind Ambleside's famous Bridge House, built allegedly to avoid traditional land tax.***

OPPOSITE: ***'Because I'm worth it!' is the cosmetic cry of competitors in the World Gurning Championship where beastliness triumphs over beauty, with a vengeance.***

where 19th-century publican Will Ritson kept his customers entertained with tall stories about the region's history.

Today, talented liars travel great distances to the Bridge Inn in Santon Bridge to spin their yarns in front of a panel of judges. The lies can be big or small – from almost believable tales of mystery and imagination involving personal encounters, to entirely believable treatises on the giant moles that formed the Lake District mountains. The great skill is the ability to tell your tale with a straight face.

Cumbrian man George Kemp has won the title twice. In 2002 George saw off nine formidable contestants with his unblinking account of entering the famous TT motorcycle race on the Isle of Man – on a balsa wood motorbike. George even stopped halfway round the course to discuss tactics with famous motor racing ace, Nigel Mansell, who just happened to be taking his dog for a walk.

The Biggest Liar competition goes from strength to strength and attracts worldwide attention. There's strict control of its amateur status, however, and professionals are banned. No politicians and lawyers then...

The Tax Bridge

Ambleside, Cumbria

A waterproof way of avoiding paying land tax is to build your house on water. In the Lakeland village of Ambleside, the enchanting Bridge House is said to have been built over water for that very purpose.

Bridge House is a tiny two-roomed cottage smack-bang on top of an arched bridge over Ambleside's Stock Beck stream. Local legend claims that it certainly was built over the stream by a tight-fisted family who did not want to pay land tax on a conventionally sited house.

The crooked two-storey building is also said to have been a summer house and apple store used by the occupants of Ambleside Hall. During the 19th century a family of eight are reputed to have lived a cramped existence inside the house.

In 1926, Bridge House was bought by a group of far-sighted local people, who gave it to the National Trust. The Trust later turned the house into their first recruitment and information centre. Today it is a gift-shop.

Bridge House attracted painters for years, including J M W Turner. It has a fair claim to being the smallest house in England, although there's a fairly big list of similar claimants. It may well be the most photographed house in the country, however.

Ugly Mugs in Egremont

Egremont, Cumbria

A pretty face counts for nothing in Egremont in September. The village's famous Crab Fayre features plenty of traditional events – Cumberland wrestling, Morris dancing, races, and a fun-fair amongst them; but in the evening, at the market hall, no beautiful people need apply when the World Gurning Championship kicks off with a grotesque grin.

The contest's rubber-faced hopefuls take turns to don a horse collar, and then twist, turn and 'gurn' their faces into ultimate ugliness. The winner is decided by the level of applause and appreciation from an enthusiastic audience. Only the British can face up to this kind of fun.

Crab Fayre was first held in 1276 to celebrate the generosity of the local Lord of the Manor who wheeled a cart of crab apples into the village and distributed them to the poor. Crab apples have a notoriously sharp taste, and the villagers may well have pulled a few funny faces as they bit into the fruit. It is from these early tales of grateful, but gurned locals that the Gurning Championship is said to have developed.

This gathering of gurners attracts media attention from all over the world, and there is even sponsorship from US companies. It's a refreshing antidote to conventional beauty contests and to the modern trend towards cosmetic 'beauty' at all costs. Gurners are gorgeous... because they're worth it...

A Far from Home Stone

Keswick, Cumbria

The 2000-tonne Bowder Stone is a long way from home and is unlikely to make it back, unless climate change introduces a new Ice Age. The enormous Bowder is roughly square-shaped and is about 10 metres (33 feet) high. It stands precariously on one corner, as if ready to topple at a touch. The stone looks like a misfit, and it is. The surrounding hills and valleys are of a very different type of rock and the Bowder Stone is not a local.

From its improbable position it is easy to imagine the Bowder bounding out of the sky with a mighty thud. But the stone is simply an Ice Age 'erratic', although there is nothing simple about the mechanics of erraticism. During the Ice Age vast slow-moving rivers of ice covered much of Britain. These carved many of the hills and valleys of today, and transported vast quantities of rock and rubble for great distances. An erratic is a lump of rock collected among the detritus hoovered up by a moving glacier. Erratics are then slowly moved along for hundreds of years to be left high and dry in a strange country when an Ice Age ends and glaciers melt. It is thought that the 'McBowder' Stone originally came from Scotland.

In the 1880s there was a serious proposal that the

ABOVE: ***The burly Bowder Stone was an Ice Age wanderer from up north, carried on the shoulders of a glacier. Global warming, or icing, may set it wandering again.***

Bowder Stone should be smashed up and the pieces used for paving old trackways, but the Big Yin, as it is affectionately called, is now in the care of the National Trust, and you can even climb onto its top, via a convenient wooden staircase.

SMILESTONES

Consett to Sunderland, Durham

Take a trip along an old railway line in Durham and a trail of 'milestone' art works will bring a smile to your face. The entertaining and thought-provoking works range from scrap metal cows and a stainless steel theodilite, to the huge head of 'King Coal' that seems to stick out of the earth.

The Stanhope and Tyne Railroad that ran between Consett and Sunderland was built in 1834 and operated during a remarkable era of Durham industry that embraced coal-mining and iron- and steel-working. These core industries declined throughout the late 20th century until the closure of the Consett Steelworks in 1985 brought closure also to the skilled workforce of the area.

When the railway became redundant, Durham County Council transformed part of the track into a cycle trail and this was extended by the SUSTRANS organization, the Sustainable Transport Charity that aims to promote cycle tracks and other ways of non-motorized transport. An imaginative part of the SUSTRANS scheme was to mark distances along the route with modern sculptures and art works that would reflect the spirit of the area's industrial past.

Today the old railway line is overlooked by a succession of marvellous works that include the *Beamish Shorthorns*, by Sally Matthews, a herd of scrap iron cows; *Terris Novalis*, by Tony Cragg, represented as a theodolite and an engineer's level, and Andy Goldsworthy's *The Lambton Earthwork*, which captures the image of the railway itself.

Perhaps the most stirring pieces are *The Old Transformers* and *King Coal*, both by David Kemp.

Created from massive industrial artefacts, *The Old Transformers* are dubbed The Ironmaster and The Miner, icons of Consett industry, while *King Coal* represents the 'giant' of coal that lies below the ground.

This is Art as metaphor, but such offbeat creations meet the criteria of more traditional follies; they may seem useless in functional terms, but they are always thought-provoking and uplifting.

Antony's Angel

Gateshead, Durham

Modern artists, like builders of great follies, strive always for the novel and the newsworthy. But the sculptor Antony Gormley stands out as a creator on the grand scale, of works that would have delighted the great folly-builders of the past.

Gormley's folly *de nos jours* is unquestionably the all-steel Angel of the North, the largest sculpture in Britain – a brilliant fusing, or in this case welding, of art, industry and social comment.

The Angel dominates the landscape of Gateshead on Tyneside, North East England. It is 20 metres (65 feet) tall; the 54-metre (177-foot) wingspan is wider than that of a Boeing 757; it weighs 200 tonnes (220 tons). The statistics are formidable, and the reality of the Angel is awesome. Initial scepticism from some quarters was soon swept aside by the Angel's sheer scale.

It is estimated that 90,000 people see the Angel every day. That means that 33 million pairs of eyes focus on its mighty presence in just one year. If Gormley were hoping to win major exposure for his work, this beats even the most determined attention-seeking Hollywood star.

Is the Angel of the North eccentric? It has to be, because of its originality and its uniqueness, but mainly because it fits the folly criteria perfectly as something that is extraordinary, apparently useless, yet exhilarating and inspiring.

The Angel has already encouraged other eccentricities. It was barely on its feet before Britain's top rock-climber, Leo Houlding, happened to be driving by, skidded to a halt and promptly climbed to the top of the Angel's head, where he stood – arms outflung. Do not attempt to emulate...

RIGHT: ***The mighty Angel of the North is a work of art that bestrides every cultural map. Let us hope it never claps its wings together.***

Wales

Wales draws you in with ease to its marvellous landscapes, its unique traditions and its rich individuality. It is a country in its own right, locked by land to England, but entirely different in every way. This is where your tongue twists round Welsh place names, such as the famous Llanfairpwllgwyngyllgogerychwyrndrobwll-llantysiliogogogoch, and where you'll find astonishing contrasts in landscape, from the awesome mountains of Snowdonia to the beautiful coast of Pembroke and the old coal-mining valleys of the south. From Cardiff Castle to the surreal village of Portmeirion, Wales has more than its fair share of strange buildings and remarkable architecture, while it is well out in front when it comes to quirky events, from ancient gatherings to the even more surreal art of bog snorkelling.

Ladies of Llangollen, Loose Legs & Llanfairpwllgwyngyllgogerychwyrndrobwllllan-tysiliogogogoch

Quirky Castles

Cardiff and Tongwynlais, Glamorgan

Old Bill the Conqueror and his hard-nosed Normans would not recognize Cardiff Castle today. They built the original, but never envisaged the marvellous makeover that two 19th-century medievalists imposed upon it.

Today's Cardiff Castle is largely the eccentric creation of the 3rd Marquess of Bute, John Patrick Crichton-Stuart, who was enthusiastically abetted by his architect, William Burges. The Marquess's family had made a fortune out of coal-exporting, and Bute's collaboration with Burges matched unlimited funds with the pair's shared enthusiasm for medievalism and Victorian Romanticism.

Cardiff Castle features a riot of Gothic, Classical and Moorish themes. There is an Arab Room designed as a fanciful harem, complete with trellised windows and sandalwood roof, and embedded with lapus lazuli and Welsh gold. Heraldry, Biblical allegory, Astrology and

LEFT: ***Cardiff Castle's mighty walls enclose a fabulous farrago of fashions in architecture, design and arts and crafts across the whole of history.***

PREVIOUS PAGE: ***Portmeirion's superb variety of building styles proves the ultimate design rule that anything goes, provided the design is right.***

Nature are major themes that ripple from room to fabulous room. Other quirky features include a bedroom that has dozens of mirrors in the ceiling, said to multiply the light from candles, and there is a wardrobe that replicates a confessional. There's a summer roof garden on a Roman theme and other splendid features include a table through which a grape vine can be trained.

Not content with turning Cardiff Castle into a marvellous cornucopia of contemporary kitsch, Bute let Burges loose on the family's ruined Castle Coch at Tongwynlais, a few kilometres north-west of the city. Burges turned Castle Coch from a stubbled ruin into a fairy-tale castle of round towers with conical roofs and medieval curtain walls, drawbridge and portcullis.

As he did with Cardiff Castle, Burges filled the interiors with a riot of heraldic motifs. Walls and domed ceilings are covered with painted butterflies, birds, monkeys and stars. Both Cardiff Castle and Castle Coch can be visited daily throughout the year.

ABOVE: *Cwmyoy's St Martin's Church, where sturdy Welsh walls and roofs have withstood the wrenching and wringing of landslips.*

Beat Generation

Laugharne, Dyfed

At the charming Welsh village of Laugharne, on the Tâf Estuary you risk a mock beating if your knowledge of local geography is not up to scratch.

Every three years on Whit Monday, the village conducts the ancient ceremony of the Common Walk. The event, also known as Beating the Bounds, is a tradition shared with many other locations in Britain.

At Laugharne large numbers of people join in the Common Walk that takes them round the old Corporation boundaries, as established by a charter of 1291. At various points along the way, a local lad is asked to give the precise name of the spot that the group stops at. If he fails to get it right he's promptly up-ended and pretend whacked three times. It's all good harmless fun and represents the importance in past times of knowing exactly where local boundaries were.

Common walkers may well end up with well-beaten feet also; this is no casual stroll. The ancient boundaries of Laugharne extend through a 20-mile circuit and the Common Walk begins at 6am and takes 12 hours to complete. When the weary walkers return to the town they make three circuits of the Market House and still manage to raise a cheer with whatever breath they have left.

The poet Dylan Thomas lived in Laugharne, but there are no poems about the Common Walk. Thomas would probably have preferred to beat the bounds round the local taverns. He is said to have modelled his fictional town of Llarregub, centrepiece of the lyrical masterpiece *Under Milk Wood* on Laugharne; although some claim that the fishing village of Mousehole in Cornwall, where Thomas and his wife Caitlin McNamara lived for a time, is the model for this entertaining verbal inversion.

Laugharne also has a fascinating old castle which has been renovated and can be visited.

A Slip of a Church

Cwmyoy, Gwent

You need to look twice at St Martin's Church at Cwmyoy in the Black Mountains; otherwise you may think that your eyes deceive you. St Martin's is a

ABOVE: *Inside Cwmyoy's St Martin's Church you might think you're on the decks of a ship at sea; even the floor is uneven.*

resilient survivor of the surrounding landscape's tendency to slip and slither all over the place. The sturdy little Gothic building looks as if giant hands have wrung it out and dropped it back in place. The tower leans drunkenly, the walls flex in the opposite direction, and masonry buttresses shore up the whole structure.

Above Cwmyoy stands the Hatterrall Ridge, along which the footpath known as Offa's Dyke winds its exhilarating way. Above Cwmyoy is the massive landslip of Graig. Here bands of heavy sandstone are separated by thinner, softer bands of marl that lie at a steep angle. When the final Ice Age de-frosted, water seeped onto the surface of the marl bands and turned them into skid pads down which the heavier sandstone masses slid. This left great gaps in the mountains that are now filled with rocky debris.

The slippery slopes are still there, and smaller landslides have contributed to St Martin's crazy appearance. The interior of the church is every bit as intriguing; an undulating slate floor rambles up to a lurching chancel arch.

Remedial work seems to have secured St Martin's, and this wonderful little building looks safely rooted in the Black Mountain earth, in spite of its eccentric appearance.

Mind Boggling in the Marsh

Llanwrtyd Wells, Powys

Dive in, the water's warm! That's invitation enough on some tropical beach or at the edge of a crystal-clear heated pool. But for a gang of daft devotees, who gather annually at the heart of a Welsh moor near Llanwrtyd Wells in Powys, taking a dip means something far more daunting than a leisurely length or two at the local Lido.

Llanwrtyd's annual World Bog Snorkelling Championships sees competitors in wet suits, masks and flippers swim two laps through a 55-metre (180-foot) trench in a peat bog. The trench is just over a metre deep. It's like swimming through tea leaves.

This mind-boggling event has been going strong for a number of years and attracts journalists, film and TV crews from all over the world. It was all started by publican Gordon Green of the Neuadd Arms, who has a flair for quirky schemes.

Responding to a competition run by a whiskey company looking for oddball ways of raising money for charities, Green came up with bog snorkelling. His idea did not win, but, flushed with enthusiasm, he staged the first World Bog Snorkelling Championships. The event drew 20 competitors and the proceeds were donated to the Llanwrtyd Wells Community Centre. It has been held each August Bank Holiday ever since, although the Foot and Mouth episode forced cancellation in 2001. Nearly 100 competitors take part and some come from as far away as Australia, the USA and Russia.

Not content with straightforward swimming, Green also introduced the Mountain Bike Bog Snorkelling World Championships in which bikers pedal madly through a deeper trench. They're allowed to surface four times for air. Anyone for tennis?...

ABOVE: *Flying the flag for international bog snorkelling at Llanwrtyd Wells, one of the world's truly outstanding eccentric events.*

Prisoner's Puzzle

Portmeirion, Gwynedd

The fabulous folly-filled village of Portmeirion on the Aber Ia peninsula, near Porthmadog, is a kind of architectural Rubik cube. Wherever you turn, you're faced with enigmas. And Portmeirion was made even more enigmatic by the maddeningly mysterious 1960s cult television series *The Prisoner*.

The Prisoner introduced a huge number of people to the delights of Portmeirion, but the village endures in its own right as the inspired creation of Bertram Clough Williams-Ellis (1883-1978), who built Portmeirion on his private estate on the coast of Snowdonia between 1925 and 1975.

Clough Williams-Ellis had an exhilarating love of landscape and of what he himself described as 'lavishness, gaiety and cultivated design'. He believed

ABOVE AND RIGHT: *Two of the many wayside accents at Portmeirion, where there is always something to intrigue the visitor round every corner.*

that human intrusion need not destroy the beauty of nature and set out to prove the point with Portmeirion. The result is, indeed, pleasing, although there is still a hint of folly-ness about the eclectic cornucopia of buildings that reflect a fascinating mix of architectural styles, from Italianate campanile to Scandinavian weather-boarding.

Modernist architects might judge Williams-Ellis's vision as overly romantic, but Portmeirion charms with its 'gaiety'. It became a natural choice for the location of *The Prisoner*, exemplar of the enigmatic, in which the actor, and creator of the series, Patrick McGoohan, played a bewildered but determined public servant known simply as No.6, who seeks to make sense of a threatening, surreal regime.

Today Portmeirion is an entirely unthreatening and charming complex, of hotel and holiday lets. The village is also open to day visitors.

The Up and Down and Up and Down Again Train

Llanberis, Gwynedd

Take a trip on the Snowdon railway and you'll probably end up with your head in the clouds. The Snowdon Mountain Railway is over 100 years old and is Britain's only rack and pinion railway. Its top station, on the summit plateau of Snowdon, is the highest station in Britain; hence the clouds – they can hardly miss the 1085-metre (3560-foot) top of the mountain.

It takes about an hour for this unique little railway to trundle up the 10 kilometres of single track. You board at sea level at the old slate-quarrying village of Llanberis and head instantly uphill towards the rocky summit.

The route is served by five steam and four diesel locomotives and three railcars. One of the steam locos dates from 1895.

Clear days are rather rare in these cloud-gathering

mountains, but the views are stupendous when visibility is good. There's a café at the summit, although on wet and windy days it's more of a Turkish bath, as crowds of passengers cram in after their obligatory stumble around the rocky summit of Snowdon in the driving mist and rain. It's a rewarding, if thoroughly eccentric experience, regardless of conditions.

Snowdon is an awesome mountain and is a rock-climbing and hill-walking paradise; but only if you have experience and are fully equipped. Do not wander too far in the mist. There are steep cliffs nearby. Let the train take you down, or walk down, wearing stout footwear and weatherproof clothing.

ABOVE: ***All aboard for a trip into the clouds on Snowdon's remarkable mountain railway.***

BELOW: ***Showing a leg for the 1st Marquess of Anglesey at Plas Newydd near Llanfair PG.***

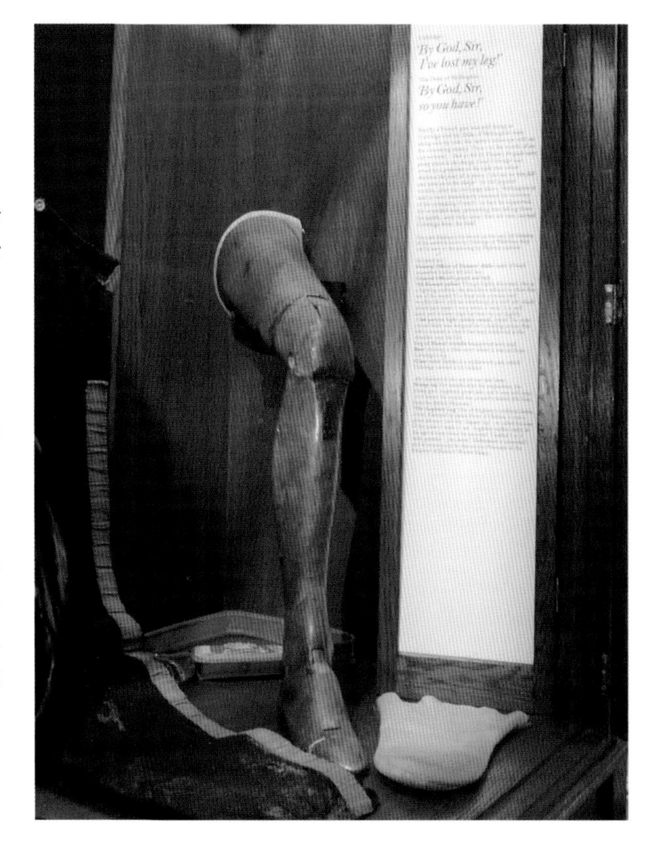

Leg Up At Llanfairpwll...Etc

Llanfair PG, Anglesey

Take a deep breath and head for Llanfairpwllgwyngyll-gogerychwyrndrobwll-llantysiliogogogoch.

This extended gallop of a name translates rather mundanely as 'The Church of St Mary in the hollow of the white hazel near the rapid whirlpool and the church of St Tysilio near a red cave'. It's usually shortened to the bite-sized Llanfair PG. The name seems to have originated as an early example of a publicity stunt, thought up by a 19th-century local shopkeeper eager to put the village on more than its fair share of the map.

Near Llanfair PG is Plas Newydd, home to the remarkable 1st Marquess of Anglesey, who, as Lord Uxbridge, was cavalry commander at the Battle of Waterloo in 1815. Paget was escorting the Duke of Wellington during the last minutes of the battle when a stray shot struck his right knee. The lower leg had to be amputated on the spot, without anaesthetic and Uxbridge had to bite down on a lump of cork. He is said to have called out to Wellington, who was studying the routed enemy through a telescope, 'By God, sir, I've lost my leg.' Glancing down with his unoccupied eye the duke is said to have responded; 'By God, sir, so you have.'

Uxbridge was soon on his foot again, cheerfully commenting that it was worth losing a leg for Waterloo. His severed limb was dutifully buried in a garden opposite the inn at Waterloo. An accompanying monument bears the inscription:

Here lies the Marquess of Anglesey's leg
Pray for the rest of his body we beg.

ABOVE: ***The other Plas Newydd is home to the Ladies of Llangollen and is a wonderful fusion of Tudor-Gothic and of dark wood interiors.***

Wellington was not as dismissive as it sounds. He made Uxbridge the 1st Marquess of Anglesey and the earl was soon stomping around on a remarkable artificial leg made of wood and steel. It had a moveable foot that was operated by catgut tendons. The device was marketed as the Anglesey Leg and also as the 'Clappe', because of the noise it made. The Marquess fathered 18 children, which has no relevance to his wooden leg whatsoever.

The famous leg is on display at Plas Newydd. This is not the Plas Newydd of the eccentric 'Ladies of Llangollen' (see this page), but a handsome 18th-century conflation of classical and Gothic architecture, set amidst fine gardens and with grand views of Snowdonia. The house contains a military museum that displays the Marquess's campaign relics, including his artificial leg. It also boasts a splendid collection of paintings by Rex Whistler. Plas Newydd is in the care of the National Trust and can be visited daily from Easter to October.

'BY GOD, SIR, I'VE LOST MY LEG.'

Marquess of Anglesey, Battle of Waterloo

'BY GOD, SIR, SO YOU HAVE.'

Duke of Wellington, Battle of Waterloo

LOVEABLE LADIES

Llangollen, Clwyd

Two top-hatted ladies from Ireland made their home at Llangollen in North Wales during the late 18th century and transformed a quiet little cottage into a centre of eccentric taste and style.

Llangollen once lay on the famous 'Dublin Road' that ran between London and the Irish ferry port of Holyhead. When the Kilkenny-based Lady Eleanor Butler and her kinswoman Sarah Ponsonby formed what was politely known at the time as 'an attachment' (they fell for each other), they took off along the Dublin Road in reverse, to escape from the disapproving eyes of friends and relatives.

Llangollen stopped them in their tracks for 50 years. It lay amid 'the beautifullest country in the world' enthused Lady B. The pair bought the little house of Plas Newydd, outside the town, and created an enchanted life, incidentally for others as much as for themselves. They lived in devoted companionship from 1780 to 1829 without a whisper of malice against them.

Splendidly eccentric in taste and attitude, the Ladies of Llangollen, as they became famously known, wore mannish riding habits and top hats when out and about. They transformed Plas Newydd into a black-and-white timbered mansion that sports Gothic protuberances such as oriole windows of stained glass. Interiors were dense with black carved oak panelling and furniture.

ABOVE: ***The mighty Pontcysyllte Aqueduct strides across the valley of the River Dee and carries canal leisure boats along a serene sky-high stream.***

Here the ladies busied themselves happily with all manner of studies and pastimes, steadily shaping their house and garden in their image. They were visited by a string of famous people, who all seem to have had a deep affection for them. Among their visitors were Charles Darwin, William Wordsworth, Sir Walter Scott, Thomas de Quincey, Lady Caroline Lamb and the Duke of Wellington.

Some writers of the day penned arch, but affectionate, pieces about the ladies, but again the pair seem to have been universally loved. Local people cherished them and their memory is revered to this day in Llangollen. Plas Newydd, with its enchanting furnishings and memorabilia, and its lovely gardens is open to the public.

Sky High Stream

Trevor Basin, Clwyd

You can take a horse to water but you can't make it swim, let alone drink. But a horse once fell into the Pontcysyllte Aqueduct on the Shropshire Union Canal and swam for its life. The fact that the aqueduct stands 38 metres (124 feet) above the valley of the River Dee and has no outer guard rail says something for horse sense.

The Pontcysyllte Aqueduct is one of the wonders of canal engineering. It carries the Llangollen section of the canal across the great trench of the Dee valley and is supported by 18 tall piers. The eastern side of the aqueduct is flanked by a towpath along which canal horses clattered, pulling behind them barges on an adjacent water-filled iron trough. Today the towpath is a pleasant walkway protected from the dizzying drop by sturdy railings.

Not so the waterway. Narrow boats steal quietly across, skimming alongside the unprotected edge of the iron trough. Cruising manuals suggest that small children and pets should be carefully escorted along the towpath, or kept safely below during the 30-metre (98-foot) crossing.

You can't help imagining a sudden rise in water levels – an overflow hardly bears thinking about – but water levels are well-regulated, of course. In its heyday the aqueduct and the Trevor Basin on the north side, saw scores of barges and their stomping horses; Slate and limestone were the main cargoes.

The Pontcysyllte Aqueduct was opened in 1805 and was built by the outstanding engineer of the day, Thomas Telford, a man who made roads, buildings, bridges and canals 'of sure, solid permanent utility', according to writer Robert Southey.

A horse did fall into the aqueduct. It broke from its tow rope and plunged in. Fortunately it decided not to scramble out the other side, but instead swam the rest of the way across. Today, you can stroll along the towpath, and from the road below you can watch modern narrow boats, often brightly decorated, steal across the aqueduct, like silent gondolas in the sky.

Scotland

Scotland is brave and beautiful – a land of rock and water, of fertile earth and deep forest, of mountains and shining sea, of bustling cities and historic towns and villages. It is a country with an awesome history, and it has been so entwined with neighbouring England that it has fundamentally shaped and influenced the greater history of Britain, yet has always had close associations with the European mainland. There is wonder in Scotland's landscapes, in the hue and texture of its buildings, and in the rich character of its people. In canny, down-to-earth Scotland the eccentric and the off-centre are not celebrated with too much enthusiasm, but there are odd buildings enough, from a full-blown Roman colosseum to a house shaped like a pineapple. The Scots impart passion to their unique festivals, from the caber-tossing of Highland Games to the mid-winter fire of Shetland's Up Helly Aa, while immortal Scottish icons such as Greyfriar's Bobby and the Loch Ness Monster continue to charm and to intrigue.

Cabers & Clavies, a Pineapple House & The Best Worst Poet in the World

HORSING ABOUT

Hawick and Selkirk, Borders

Frontiers are always lawless lands; their only common ground are the graveyards of those who fought over them. During the Middle Ages the Scottish Borders seethed with battles and blood feuds and with the theft of fat cattle, especially from the rich pastures of neighbouring England.

Home ground was often just as vulnerable to the cattle thieves, or reivers, as they were known, and Border towns would often send armed riders to patrol their boundaries, or Marches, to prevent encroachment by lawless bands and unscrupulous neighbouring landlords

Long after the Borders had been pacified and the reivers were no more, the practice of riding the boundaries survived and became known as the Common Riding. Today, many of the Border towns celebrate their rich history and culture with huge gatherings of riders during June and July. These spectacular cavalcades are always led by an unmarried man, who carries the town flag, or standard, along the route. The position is one of great honour and responsibility. Celebrations can last for a few days or a couple of weeks and truly spectacular Ridings take place at the towns of Hawick and Selkirk.

At Hawick, the most exciting feature of the Riding takes place on the second day when the principal man, known as The Cornet, leads his followers in a wild chase at full gallop to commemorate the capture of an English flag in 1514. Selkirk Common Riding is one of the oldest of the Border festivals. Over 400 riders take part and it is among the largest equestrian gatherings in Europe. The Border reivers may be long gone, but the colour and spectacle of the Ridings still manage to capture some of the spirit of those wild days.

HOME IS WHERE THE HEART MIGHT BE

Melrose, Borders

Scotland's immortal hero Robert the Bruce had a well-travelled heart. After his death, in 1329, his heart was carted off towards the Holy Land by his right-hand man, Sir James Douglas, known as Black Douglas – a man who was thought by his enemies to be entirely heartless.

Douglas carried Bruce's heart in a casket round his neck. He got as far as Andalucía in southern Spain where he was killed by Muslim forces; but not before he threw Bruce's heart at them. The heart was recovered and brought back to Scotland to be buried under the Chapter House floor of Melrose Abbey.

Mystery hovers over Bruce's heart, however. It

ABOVE: ***Melrose Abbey where Robert the Bruce's heart found a final resting place.***

OPPOSITE: ***A heart of stone at Melrose Abbey commemorates Robert the Bruce.***

certainly went missing from his body. Bruce was buried at Dunfermline Abbey and in 1818 his skeleton was exhumed. It was found that the ribs had been cut through, suggesting that the heart was probably removed, a common practice in those days, when hearts of notable people were often preserved elsewhere.

The heart seems to have been placed in a Russian doll sequence of lead caskets, one inside the other. In 1996, archaeologists investigated. They drilled a hole through the shell of Bruce's casket and had a peek inside, using a fibre- optic cable camera. They found another conical casket bearing a plate that indicated it had been opened by investigators in 1921. Not much else has been disclosed, but a spokesperson hedged round the matter with the masterful obfuscation of all good scientists: 'It is reasonable to assume that it was Bruce's heart,' he said.

ABOVE: ***Even the stoniest heart would surely melt at the story of Greyfriars' Bobby; devoted dog or daily diner?***

PAGE 141: ***Giving it stick in a very big way during a Highland Games' caber tossing competition.***

The casket was reburied in 1998 and on the anniversary of Bruce's 1314 victory over the English King Edward II at Bannockburn, an inscribed stone, bearing a carving of a heart, was unveiled at Melrose.

Dogged Devotion

Edinburgh, Lothian

Every dog has its day, but Edinburgh's famous Greyfriars Bobby took a grip on immortality by making every day a day of devotion to his dead master.

It's enough to make you weep; but the tale of Bobby, the soulful Skye terrier, could melt granite. Today, a likeness of Bobby adorns a fountain outside Greyfriars Churchyard, the oldest burial ground in Edinburgh. People come from all over the world to be photographed next to the statue, and a film was even made about Bobby.

Those who love dogs unconditionally would claim that Bobby's devotion to his dead master says everything about canine fidelity. Cynics might say he was just looking for lunch.

Bobby's story is a simple one. He was the companion of a man called John Gray who died in 1858 and was buried in the churchyard of Greyfriars. Bobby was at the graveside on the day of the burial, and was there every day thereafter, regardless of the weather.

The man who looked after the graveyard took pity on the little dog and began to feed him. This may confirm the cynic's view that Bobby was simply out to lunch, but there seems no doubt that the terrier had a genuine and long-lasting devotion to his dead master. He hung around Gray's graveside for 14 years until his own death in 1872.

Bobby's devotion caught the imagination of contemporary Edinburgh, a place not famous for being too sentimental about its human inhabitants; but in 1873 the statue and fountain that remain to this day were unveiled. The rest is Walt Disney...

Fabulous Fruitery

Dunmore, Stirling

India's Taj Mahal may have a head start when it comes to majestic domes, but Scotland takes the crown (or the pineapple) when it comes to topping off a building with a flourish.

The remarkable Pineapple House at Dunmore near Stirling is a magnificent summer house built in the shape of a pineapple by the 4th Earl of Dunmore in 1777. The earl was Britain's Royal Governor of Virginia just before the American Revolution. He had his hands full; what with troublesome Shawnee Indians, unhappy black slaves and rebellious white 'patriots' who were dissatisfied with British rule.

Dunmore was a pragmatist, although he was a touch eccentric and headlong when turning sensible ideas into actions. He made peace with the Shawnee, but stirred revolutionary feelings when he abolished the Virginia Assembly, among whose members was Thomas Jefferson. But it was Dunmore's action in freeing black slaves so that they could fight in the British Army that

Velcro Man!

South Queensferry, Lothian

In hot August, just imagine covering yourself from head to toe with burrs (the sticky seedcases of the burdock plant), and then walking seven miles round town without a murmur.

This is the duty, on the second Friday in August each year, of the celebrated Burry Man of the old fishing village of South Queensferry on the Firth of Forth. The Burry Man is extraordinary; more so because he speaks not a word as he walks (with some difficulty, it has to be said), his arms outstretched, each hand holding a staff covered in flowers.

So sticky are the burrs that the Burry Man's legs would weld together if they touched. So he waddles the dawdle, rather than walks the walk. Two attendants support his arms as he goes through the crowded town from pub to pub, where he fuels up on whisky through a straw. He's not in a hurry, the Burry Man.

Just preparing this remarkable costume is an event in its own right. The chosen bearer puts on stout clothing, then dons vest and long-johns. His head is protected by a knitted Balaclava helmet with holes for eyes, nose and mouth and the adhesive burrs are then carefully stuck to every part of his costume. A flag is wrapped round his waist and a bowler hat, covered with burrs and decorated with flowers, is placed on his head.

Fortunately for the rest of us the Burry Man has to be a native of Queensferry. Yet there's quite a queue of volunteers for the honour. Tradition states that the Burry Man must make an appearance the day before the annual Ferry Fair, which then benefits from his blessing. The origins of the tradition are uncertain, but it is centuries old and may hark back to fertility festivals. Several other Scottish fishing villages once had similar events and there is a legend of a king who hid from his enemies bundled up in burrs.

South Queensferry quite rightly treasures its Burry Man and there's even a life- sized model in the town museum. High above the village the two great bridges of the River Forth slice across the sky, heedless of ancient custom.

really inflamed the dissenters and helped precipitate violent revolt. Caught up in the early battles of the revolutionary war, Dunmore's British forces were defeated and in 1783 the earl fled from America.

Dunmore was sentimental about his days in Virginia, however. He had been amused by a homecoming custom of Virginian sailors, whereby they placed a pineapple on the gatepost of their home to announce to all and sundry that they were back. On his return to Scotland Dunmore ordered the addition of a huge pineapple dome on a small classical pavilion on his estate.

The dome was a brilliant piece of structural engineering. The architraves of the lower building were extended to encompass the stony shoots and prickly leaves of a huge stone pineapple that rises nearly 14 metres (46 feet) into the air.

Today the Pineapple, and the adjoining gardens of Dunmore, are in the care of the National Trust for Scotland and the Pineapple's flanking buildings are holiday lets managed by the Landmark Trust.

Fry Me to Mars

The Heart of Scotland

The best Scottish cuisine is of world-class quality; but the country's culinary image is stuck belly-deep in grease. There's nothing wrong with a good haggis, but the Scots' predilection for fried food argues more of haute cholesterol than cuisine. And in recent years nothing has fattened up the image of the country's dire diet more so than the deep-fried chocolate Mars Bar. The thought of it alone might fry the blood in the veins of a vegetarian.

Looked at with Scottish pragmatism, dipping a chocolate bar in batter and then popping it into a sizzling pan of cooking oil is perfectly reasonable. They've done it to fish, meat, potatoes, doughnuts, and pizzas, so why not chocolate? It's alarmingly tasty.

No one knows exactly when and where the first Mars Bar was deep-fried, but the Scottish east coast town of Stonehaven is said to have been the place. The idea certainly spread quicker than molten chocolate

ABOVE: *Fruit topping at its most spectacular graces Dunmore's famous Pineapple House near Stirling.*

RIGHT: *Frying tonight – along with fish & chips is Scotland's bid for culinary craziness, deep fried Mars Bars. Delicious, if not entirely a dietician's delight.*

ABOVE: ***Just some of the marvellous artefacts hiding within St Conan's Church on the banks of Loch Awe.***

and is now a fixed favourite. It was even tried out in France, where one Scots chef floated the dish at his top-end restaurant in Paris. It sparked a national debate, even though he had added a sprinkling of cinnamon. French culinary sensibilities were just too bruised by the battering.

Purists insist that deep-fried chocolate should be eaten with chips, but the more fastidious may settle for ice cream. Now there's a deep frying challenge...

There is some despair among health professionals about Scotland's bonny-done-dieting attitude to food and health. The Scots' health record is not good. Some parts of the country have the highest incidence of heart disease and tooth-decay in the developed world and determined efforts are underway to change hearts, minds and tastes towards following a healthier diet of fruit and vegetables. Anyone for deep-fried lettuce?

Holy Hobby

Loch Awe, Argyll

On the banks of the handsome Loch Awe is a cornucopia of a kirk. This is the remarkable St Conan's, the creation of a man with a dedicated soul, more than a dash of creative eccentricity, and the time and money to indulge his whims.

Walter Douglas Campbell was the younger brother of the 1st Lord Blythswood. Younger brothers of moneyed families are often at a loose end. Not so Walter. He was an accomplished architect and wood-carver, and an avid collector of artefacts and works of art. He bought Innischonam, an island in Loch Awe, and promptly built himself a stately home amidst the motifs of a Landseer painting. Thereafter he was never at a loose end.

Walter settled on the island with his sister and his mother and the story goes that the elder Mrs Campell, a regular church-goer, was fed up with the long drive to church in Dalmally. Walter decided to build her a more convenient kirk and spent the rest of his life creating what is now St Conan's. In 1907 he began the conversion of an existing Victorian church, a fairly modest building of 1886 that is now absorbed by the present church.

It was a long job. Walter designed every part of what became a highly eclectic building that displays numerous styles of architecture, from ancient standing stones to Saxon, Norman, and Romanesque features. The result is enchanting.

The stone used for the building was gleaned from the open hill; every piece of natural stone had to be cut and shaped on the spot. Beauty before symmetry was Douglas Campbell's watchword. He was meticulous and patient, and often pulled down features that he felt were not quite right, rebuilding them again and again. The southern façade of the church is particularly handsome; the main tower is Saxon and has decorated stonework. There is a smaller French-style tower and a number of motifs, including lively gargoyles.

The interior of St Conan's is even more elaborate. Here, Campbell incorporated numerous materials and artefacts that he had collected over the years, including slabs of marble from the Levant, oak beams from two old battleships, a bell from the Skerryvore lighthouse, screens from Eton College, seats from various Edinburgh churches, and a chair from Venice.

Walter Douglas Campbell died in 1914, but his sister continued to fulfil his dream of what must surely

be described as a religious folly, given that St Conan's eschewed function for creativity. The result is entirely fruitful.

ABOVE: ***When in Rome – or Oban for that matter – do as the Romans do. In this case, banker Stuart McCaig just had to build himself a colosseum in the West Highlands.***

Roman In The Gloamin'

Oban, Argyll

The Romans never got to Oban, so the remarkable colosseum known as McCaig's Folly that dominates the town may seem a little bit odd.

McCaig's Folly is of course a more recent structure than Rome's famous Flavian Amphitheatre of AD 70–82. It is an impressive piece of work all the same and is another example of Victorian grandiosity and the compulsion to build follies that gripped 19th-century grandees.

Stuart McCaig was a successful local banker who set about building his own private colosseum in 1897 inspired in equal parts by egotism and philanthropy.

The late 19th century was a time of high unemployment in the Argyle area, and McCaig conceived the folly as a job creation scheme for the idling stonemasons of Oban. He spent £5000 on the project – an enormous sum at the time – and intended the folly to be a monument to himself and his family.

Like many Victorians McCaig was gripped by the spirit of Empire and was seduced by Greek and Roman architecture. He had travelled widely in Italy and, inspired by the buildings that he had seen there, decided to build his own colosseum.

Stuart McCaig died before his scheme was completed. In his will he provided several thousand pounds to be made available each year until the job was done, but his sister Catherine successfully challenged the will and won the day; the judges referred to Stuart

McCaig as an 'eccentric testator'. The colosseum and its planned central tower were therefore never completed, and the intended statues of McCaig's ancestors never took their places in the apertures. Thus on two counts, grandiose uselessness and failure, McCaig's colosseum fits the definition of a folly.

The colosseum is still an impressive building, although the people of Oban may be forgiven for being a touch irritated at their town being so visibly dominated. But then Oban has enough attractions and qualities to outweigh a monument to one man's wealthy indulgence. And the views from the hilltop site are spectacular, with or without a folly.

Worse Verse

Dundee, Angus

Most people believe they have a book in them. Exactly where it is can prove elusive, of course; but if you can't find your inner book, then usually a verse or two will do. Even so, the skills of great poetry accrue to but a few, while the skills of being a good bad poet are rare indeed.

'...THE SAVING GRACE OF ECCENTRICITY DESCENDED UPON HIM...'

Norman MacCaig on William McGonagall

The world's best worst poet ever, was probably Sir William Topaz McGonagall, Poet and tragedian, Knight of the White Elephant (Burma), McGonagall was born in Edinburgh in 1825 and was of Irish descent. He became a weaver in Dundee on the brisk east coast of Scotland.

There was nothing brisk about William's poetry. He wrote long rambling lines of tormented meter and tortured rhyme. His subjects were epic; his poems pathetic, yet McGonagall is famous because his talent for writing bad verse was unique. His verse has an almost hypnotic quality.

McGonagall also possessed the essential characteristic of the true eccentric: he was utterly convinced of his worth as a poet and actor. Norman MacCaig, one of Scotland's genuinely accomplished poets, once said, without malice, that McGonagall must have been quite a bore, but that 'the saving grace of eccentricity descended upon him' Poor William was the butt of jokes and hoaxes throughout his life, although he enjoyed enormous publicity and his 'works' were published regularly in local papers and magazines.

Local students were McGonagall's most merciless fans. They encouraged the innocent poet in his hilarious performances, at which, without fail, a barrage of rotten fruit and vegetables would rain down on the stage. They hoaxed William into meetings with famous people, as impersonated by one of their number, and they convinced him that he had been awarded the entirely bogus title of Knight of the White Elephant, from an admiring King Theebaw of the Andaman Islands.

ABOVE: ***The great bridge that spans the River Tay between the city of Dundee and the county of Fife inspired the deathless poetry of William McGonagall.***

The blessed Mc Gonagall survived it all. He even managed to raise a subscription to take him to America 'on tour', although once back in Scotland his precarious life, and that of his family, continued. He died in 1902 in Edinburgh and was buried in a pauper's grave.

Bad poets are often prolific and McGonagall was no exception. He churned out deathly poesy on every subject imaginable although he is best known for his epic lines on the Tay Bridge – one of the wonders of the Railway Age.

'Beautiful Railway Bridge of the Silvery Tay!' chirruped McGonagall on the triumphant opening of the bridge in 1878. The poet implored the Fates to ensure that no accident should ever befall the bridge:

For that would be most awful to be seen,
Near by Dundee and the Magdalen Green.

Eighteen months later, the bridge collapsed during a violent winter storm, taking a train with it, and 70 passengers to their deaths. McGonagall intoned,'Oh! Ill-fated Bridge of the Silv'ry Tay...' You can hum the rest...

Capering Cabers

Braemar, Aberdeenshire

Try picking up a tree trunk that is nearly 6 metres (19 feet) long and weighs 52 kilograms (114 pounds). Hold it upright cupped in your hands, start running, and then heave it in the air to make it land straight ahead (at 12 o' clock precisely). This is the art of caber-tossing, and if you think it sounds caber crazy, then you do not understand the remarkable character of Scotland's Highland Games. Tossing a tree trunk is the least of it.

Highland Games take place at several venues throughout Scotland. The most famous are probably the Braemar Games, chiefly because to the world's media they are the ones attended by Britain's Royal Family. Braemar also boasts the biggest cabers of all. But all Highland Games are prestigious affairs.

The Highland Games as portrayed today originated during the 19th century when a gallimaufry of Sir Walter Scott romanticism and royal sentimentality spawned organized events at which traditional Highland sports, such as hammer-throwing, caber-tossing and stone-putting, led the field, with running, jumping and Highland dancing thrown in.

RIGHT: ***The Highland Games focus on genuine power sports, from tossing the caber to heaving the hammer.***

ABOVE: ***Check out those magnificent 'tackety boots' as this Highland Games tug-o'-war team puts heart and 'sole' into it, in more ways than one.***

There were always sports and pastimes in the Highlands, however. Clans often staged feats of strength, mock sword fights and wrestling matches as a raw kind of training for the serious business of mayhem that was an inescapable part of life. This was probably formalized at times, with a general air of festivity; but a 14th-century king once staged a thorough blood bath of an 'entertainment' that would horrify today's be-kilted royals.

In 1396, on the open ground known as the North Inch at Perth, King Robert III arranged a pitched battle between 30 men from each of the rival clans, the MacPhersons and the Davidsons. They had been feuding for some time and Robert had failed to reconcile them. He ordered a kind of honour match for the entertainment of himself, his queen, Annabella and his courtiers.

Whether or not Robert envisaged a gentlemanly contest of Norman-like chivalry, is not known. In the event everyone went bananas and by the final whistle, 29 Davidsons and 19 MacPhersons lay dead. Stick to caber –tossing…

THE VERY VERY BIG YIN

Cairngorm Mountains, Aberdeenshire

The world's favourite Scottish comedian, Billy Connolly, may well be known as the Big Yin, but Scotland has an even bigger Yin in the shape of *Am Fear Liath Mor*, the Great Grey Man of Ben Macdhui.

The Grey Man is a huge cloudy giant that is said to

haunt the lonely heights of the Cairngorms at the heart of Scotland's Grampian Mountains. This is haunting in high places; Ben Macdhui is Britain's second highest mountain after Ben Nevis. The latter is 1343 metres (4406 feet) high; Macdhui is 1310 metres (4297 feet) high; there's a mere hop in height between the two, and one 19th-century landowner floated the idea of building a 35-metre (115 –foot) high stone pyramid on top of Macdhui, just to belittle Nevis.

The Grey Man may or may not have approved of the idea. He takes the form of a huge shadowy figure seen – usually at a distance – across the sweeping vistas of the high plateaux. Some claim that the apparition is accompanied by the thudding sound of giant feet, especially in winter as *Am Fear Liath Mor* clumps across the snow fields.

Ghosts are usually conveniently inexplicable; but what makes the Grey Man fascinating is that here is one 'ghost' that is easily explained by cold physics. The Grey Man is nothing more than a magnified projection of the observer's own figure on clouds that are at the same level as the observer, an explanation that also explains why some reports of the Grey Man describe how he stops every time the observer stops. He would, wouldn't he?

Ghost enthusiasts will dress up *Am Fear Liath Mor* as much more of a Bigfoot-type figure with distinct characteristics; but the cloud figure explanation is well attested. The phenomenon is called the Brocken Spectre, after a peak in Germany's Harz Mountains where configurations of landscape and low-flying cloud often produce such chimera. A more common name for the phenomenon is a 'glory' and it is caused by sunlight projecting the shadow of an observer onto clouds. It creates a remarkable same-size image that is encircled by a rainbow aureole. But no one will ever believe what you just saw...

ABOVE: ***The Loch Ness Monster is an enduringly bizarre beast. The eyes – and the camera – may well deceive, but Nessy-watching remains compulsive.***

Not Necessarily Nessie

Loch Ness, Invernesshire

If you go down to Loch Ness today...you could be in for a disappointment.

Dedicated Loch Ness watchers are never put off, of course, from the hope of spotting one of the world's most enduring, elusive and downright eccentric of mythological creatures.

Simply using the word 'myth' in relation to the famous Loch Ness Monster marks anyone down as an unforgivable sceptic, so much is Nessie held in affection. The marvellous enigma about enigmas of this nature is that they are extremely difficult to disprove.('There are more things in heaven and earth, Horatio...' *Hamlet.)*

The Legend of the Loch Ness Monster probably has its roots in the ancient legends that hovered round a hundred misty lochs in the always mysterious Highlands of Scotland. The modern Nessie was first 'spotted' in 1932 by a couple who were driving along a new road on the north side of the loch. This new road

ABOVE: ***Scratching the surface of the Loch Ness Monster Legend; there are many alleged incidents of Nessie caught on camera, but this is a story that will always surface.***

gave panoramic views of the great expanse of water that slices its way through the Great Glen. The pair claimed to have seen a large creature breaking the surface of the loch. Newspaper reports immediately used the word 'monster' and Nessie, as a larger-than-life phenomenon, was born. Another report of the 'monster' being seen on land soon followed. Then, in 1934, a photograph surfaced, purporting to be an image of a long-necked Nessie; the picture remained a Nessie icon for 60 years until its dramatic exposure as a clever fake.

Dedicated monster-spotting continues unabated, however. Photographs of dubious-looking disturbances on the surface of the loch appear regularly, and scientific investigations using state of the art sonar and underwater photography have been exhaustive, but inconclusive.

It is likely that most Nessie sightings are illusions, fuelled by wishful thinking. Among the many Nessie lookalikes are large branches and sudden flurries of wind that can almost sculpt the surface of the water into distinctive 'whalebacks' and spirals. Hoaxes flourish. One cheerful jape was often set up by the crews of fishing boats and small coasters passing through the Loch Ness section of the Caledonian Canal. Crews used to rope together old tyres and boxes in creative mode, and then slip them over the side of their vessels at night, ready for the avid glitter from scores of roadside binoculars in the morning light.

Barrels of Fiery Fun In Burghead

Burghead, Moray

Sparks really do fly in the Scottish harbour town of Burghead on the 11th January. At one time New Year's Eve or Hogmanay, was celebrated on the 11th January before changes were made to the calendar in 1660. But why spoil a good thing? In Burghead the traditional, fiery way of seeing in the New Year, the Burning of the Clavie, was retained on the 11th and it still takes place in plenty of time for modern New Year hangovers to have subsided.

Clavie is a word to roll round the tongue; it derives from the Gaelic *cliabh,* meaning 'basket' and was the name given to an old herring barrel that was filled with wood shavings and tar and then set alight. Nowadays an iron-hooped whisky barrel is used. Once emptied of its usual fiery contents, it is daubed with creosote, and then fired up. Traditionally, the spark comes from a smouldering lump of peat taken from the hearth of a past provost of the town, and the clavie is carried from the house by the elected Clavie King.

About ten local men – traditionally they should be fishermen – are chosen each year to take turns carrying the flaming barrel clockwise around the town. They stop at the homes of eminent citizens to present a glowing ember from the clavie, an act that is said to confer good luck upon the household. Eventually the procession makes its way through the chilly winter night to a stone altar in the old fort on Doorie Hill, where the clavie is set down. More fuel is added until a roaring bonfire lights up the hill. Embers from the fire are gathered by onlookers who use them to kindle lucky New Year fires at home.

The origins of the event are a mystery. Pictish and Roman connections have been cited, but a Norse origin is likely.

Burning Your Boats In Lerwick

Lerwick, Shetland

In the Shetland Islands they don't so much shiver their timbers as set them alight in one of Europe's most spectacular end-of-the year ceremonies, Lerwick's famous Up Helly Aa. Even the name conjures up a sense of heat.

On the last Tuesday in January Lerwick is packed with revellers, known as Guizers, in fancy dress and others dressed as wild-looking Viking warriors. A full-sized Viking longship is torched along the way. Yet, despite appearances, and despite Shetland's strong connections with Norse history and culture, Up Helly Aa is a purely Scottish19th century invention.

There had been January celebrations in the islands for centuries, but the particularly wild goings-on from which Up Helly Aa has developed postdate the Napoleonic Wars rather than the Norse Wars. They originated in the wild carousing of sailors and soldiers returning home from war service.

In 1824 a visiting Methodist missionary reported grimly that on 'Old Christmas Eve' he had encountered outrageous and unseemly behaviour that included horn-blowing, drum-beating, firing of guns and 'shouting, bawling, fiddling, fife-ing, drinking, fighting'. It went on all night, of all things. Over the years, as Lerwick expanded, the annual celebration became bigger and rowdier, and in 1840 Burghead's burning barrels tradition was added. The town council attempted to control proceedings, but with limited success.

Then, in the early 1870s, a group of imaginative young men, keenly aware of their Norse heritage, came up with the name Up Helly Aa and introduced a torchlight procession and later a symbolic Viking longship. By the early 1900s a leading character, the Guizer Jarl, was introduced, followed a few years later by a gang of fellow Vikings.

It's been an Up Helly Aa of a night ever since. The event attracts huge numbers of visitors from outside the Shetlands, proving that when it comes to ancient festivals you never know what time-honoured 'tradition' is only a few steps ahead of you, all lit up and ready for a hell of a time…

BELOW: ***A formidable front of fiery fellows leads the way for Lerwick's Up Helly Aa longship on the warmest – and coldest – night of the Shetland year.***

Recommended Reading

Rogers, Byron *An Audience With An Elephant*, Aurum Press, 2001

Donaldson *William Brewer's Rogues, Villains & Eccentrics*, Cassell, 2002

Hawkes, Jacquetta *A Guide to the Prehistoric and Roman Monuments in England And Wales*, Chatto & Windus, 1951

Keay, John *Eccentric Travellers*, John Murray, 1982

le Vay, Benedict *Eccentric Britain*, Bradt Publications, 2000

Pevsner, Nicholas *The Pevsner Architectural Guides*, Penguin Press

Quinn, Tom *Tales of the Country Eccentrics*, David & Charles, 1996

Further Information

Dartmoor National Park Authority
Parke, Bovey Tracey
Newton Abbot
Devon TQ13 9JQ
Tel: 01626 832093
Fax: 01626 834684
Email: hq@dartmoor-npa.gov.uk
www.dartmoor-npa.gov.uk

English Heritage
Customer Services Department
PO Box 569
Swindon SN2 2YP
Tel: 0870 333 1181
Fax: 01793 414926
Email:
customers@english-heritage.org.uk
www.english-heritage.org.uk

Exmoor National Park Authority
Tel: 01398 323665
Fax: 01398 323150
E-mail:
info@exmoor-nationalpark.gov.uk
www.exmoor-nationalpark.gov.uk

The Landmark Trust
Shottesbrooke, Maidenhead
Berkshire SL6 3SW
Tel: 01628 825925
Fax: 01628 825417
www.landmarktrust.co.uk

The National Trust
36 Queen Anne's Gate
London SW1H 9AS
Tel: 0870 609 5380
Fax: 020 7222 5097
www.nationaltrust.org.uk

The National Trust for Scotland
5 Charlotte Square
Edinburgh EH2 4DU
Tel: 0131 226 5922
Email: information@nts.org.uk
www.nts.org.uk

CORNWALL & DEVON

CORNWALL

End to Enders
The Administration Office
Land's End John o' Groats Club
Custom House
Land's End
Sennen, Penzance
Cornwall TR19 7AA
Tel: 01736 871501
www.landsend-landmark.co.uk/enders.html

Logan Rock, Treen
See National Trust details

The Merry Maidens, Lamorna
www.stonepages.com/england/merrymaidens.html

Flora Dance, Helston
Helston Tourist Information
Tel: 01326 565431
Fax: 01326 572803
www.go-cornwall.com

May Day Obby Oss Ceremony
Padstow Tourist Information
Tel: 01841 533449
Fax: 01841 532356
www.padstowlive.com

Vicar of Morwenstow
See National Trust details

DEVON

Lydford Gorge, Dartmoor
See National Trust details

Ten Commandments Stone, Buckland-in-the-Moor
See Dartmoor National Park Authority details

Castle Drogo
Drewsteignton
nr Exeter EX6 6PB
Tel: 01647 433306
Fax: 01647 433186
See National Trust details

Widecombe Fair, Widecombe
See Dartmoor National Park Authority details

Hunting the Earl of Rone
Combe Martin Tourist Information
Tel: 01271 883319 / 882366
Fax: 01271 883319

Devil's Stone, Shebbear
Okehampton Tourist Information
Tel: 01837 53020
www.okehamptondevon.co.uk

The Gnome Reserve
West Putford
Nr Bradworthy
North Devon EX22 7XE
Tel/Fax: 0870 845 9012
Email: info@gnomereserve.co.uk
www.gnomereserve.co.uk

A la Ronde
Summer Lane
Exmouth EX8 5BD
Tel: 01395 265514
See National Trust details

SOMERSET, DORSET & WILTSHIRE

SOMERSET

Oare Village, Exmoor
See Exmoor National Park Authority details

Big Cat, Exmoor
See Exmoor National Park Authority details

Fyne Court
Broomfield
Bridgwater TA5 2EQ
Tel: 01823 451587
See National Trust details

Follies of Barwick Park, Yeovil
Yeovil Tourist Information

Tel: 01935 462991 / 2
Fax: 01935 434065
www.country-breaks.com

Wells Cathedral
Cathedral Offices, Chain Gate
Cathedral Green, Wells
Somerset BA5 2UE
Tel: 01749 674483
Fax: 01749 832210
Email: office@wellscathedral.uk.net
www.wellscathedral.org.uk

DORSET

World Nettle-eating Championship
Bottle Inn, Marshwood
Dorset DT6 5QJ
Tel: 01297 678 254
www.thebottleinn.co.uk

Cerne Abbas Giant, Giant's Hill
Dorcester Tourist Information
Tel: 01305 267992
Fax: 01305 266079

The Great Globe
Durlston Country Park
Lighthouse Road, Swanage
Dorset BH19 2JL
Tel: 01929 424443
Fax: 01929 424443
Email: info@durlston.co.uk
www.durlston.co.uk

WILTSHIRE

Stourhead House
Stourhead Estate Office, Stourton
Warminster BA12 6QD
Tel: 01747 841152
Fax: 01747 842005
See National Trust details on p154

Marquess of Bath
The Estate Office, Longleat
Warminster, Wiltshire BA12 7NW
Tel: 01985 844400
Fax: 01985 844885
Email: enquiries@longleat.co.uk
www.longleat.co.uk

SURREY, OXFORDSHIRE & BERKSHIRE

SURREY

Prospect Tower
Leith Hill, Coldharbour
Tel: 01306711777
Fax: 01306 712153
See National Trust details on p154

Watts Chapel
Down Lane, Compton, Guildford
Open during daylight hours. An guide book can be purchased from the nearby Watts Gallery
www.wattsgallery.org.uk

OXFORDSHIRE

The White Horse, Uffington Hill
See National Trust details on p154

Faringdon Folly, Faringdon Hill
Faringdon Tourist Information
Tel: 01367 242191
www.faringdon.org

Gargoyles, Oxford
Oxford Tourist Information
Tel: 01865 726871
Fax: 01865 240261

Shark House
2 New High Street
Headington, Oxford
www.headington.org.uk

Rollright Stones
The Friends of the Rollright Stones
PO Box 444
Bicester OX25 4AT
www.rollrightstones.co.uk

BERKSHIRE

Garter Ceremony
Windsor Castle
Ticket Sales & Information Office
Official Residences of the Queen
London SW1A 1AA
Tel: 020 7766 7304
Fax: 020 7930 9625
E-mail: information@royalcollection.org.uk

HAMPSHIRE & SUSSEX

HAMPSHIRE

Garlic Festival, Isle of Wight
Island Partners Ltd.
PO Box 24, Sandown
Isle of Wight PO36 9ZJ
Tel: 01983 863566
Email: garlicfestival@islandpartners.co.uk
www.garlicfestival.co.uk

Trusty Servant pub
Minstead, Hampshire SO43 7FY
Tel: 02380 812137

Highclere Castle
Newbury, Berkshire RG20 9RN
Tel: 01635 253204
Fax: 01635 255315
Email:
theoffice@highclerecastle.co.uk
www.highclerecastle.co.uk

Farley Mount Horse Mausoleum
Farley Mount Country Park
Crab Wood Depot
Sarum Road, Winchester
Hampshire SO22 5QS
Tel/Fax: 01962 860948
www.hants.gov.uk/countryside/fmcp

SUSSEX

Bognor Birdman Competition
International Bognor Birdman
Arun Civic Centre
Maltravers Road, Littlehampton
West Sussex BN17 5LF
Tel: 01903 737500
Fax: 01903 725254
Email: birdman@arun.gov.uk
www.birdman.org.uk

World Lawnmower Racing Championship
The British Lawn Mower Racing Association
Hunt Cottage, Wisborough Green
West Sussex RH14 0HN
Email: info@blmra.co.uk
www.media@blmra.co.uk

World Marble Championship
Greyhound pub, Radford Road,
Tinsley Green, West Sussex
Tel: 01403 730 602
Email: marblesam@hotmail.com

The Royal Pavilion
Brighton BN1 1EE
Tel: 01273 290900
Fax: 01273 292821
Email: visitor.services@brighton-hove.gov.uk
www.royalpavilion.org.uk

London to Brighton Veteran Car Run
Brighton & Hove City Council
Tel: 01273 292711

Bonfire Night, Lewes
Lewes Tourist Information
Tel: 01273 483448
Fax: 01273 484003
www.visit-lewes.co.uk

Fuller's Follies, Brightling
Battle Tourist Information
Tel: 01424 773721
Fax: 01424 773436
www.battletown.co.uk

Town Crier's Contest, Hastings
Battle Tourist Information
(See above)

LONDON & KENT

LONDON

Tower of London
London EC3N 4AB
Tel: 0870 756 6060
www.hrp.org.uk

Clink Prison Museum
1 Clink Street
London SE1 9DG
Tel: 020 7403 9000
www.clink.co.uk

London Eye
South Bank
Tel: 0870 5000 600
www.londoneye.com

Pearly Kings and Queens Procession to St Martin's-in-the-Field, Trafalgar Square
Visit London
Tel: 020 7932 2000
Fax: 020 7932 0222
Email: enquiries@visitlondon.com
www.visitlondon.com

Sir John Soane's Museum
Lincoln's Inn Fields
13 Lincoln's Inn Fields
London WC2A 3BP
Tel: 020 7405 2107
Fax: 020 7831 3957
www.soane.org

Serpentine swimmers, Hyde Park
Serpentine Swimming Club
Alan Titmuss, General Secretary
Tel: 01344 291 578
Email: AlanTitmuss@aol.com
www.serpentineswimmingclub.com

Chiswick House
Burlington Lane
ChiswickW4
Tel: 020 8995 0508
See English Heritage details on p154

Sir Richard Burton's Grave
St. Mary Magdalene's Church
61 North Worple Way, Mortlake
Tel: 020 8876 1326
Open 9am-4pm

Severndroog Castle
Castlewood, Shooter's Hill SE18
Greenwich Tourist Information
Tel: 0870 608 2000
www.greenwich.gov.uk

KENT

Margate Cave
1, Northdown Road
Cliftonville, Margate
Kent CT9 1QQ
Tel: 01843 220 139
Fax: 01843 834 428
www.aboutbritain.com

ESSEX, SUFFOLK & NORFOLK

ESSEX

Mud Race, Maldon
Maldon Tourist Information
Tel: 01621 856 503
www.maldon.gov.uk

Thaxted Ring Meeting
Thaxted CM6
Contact David Brewster
Tel: 01245 420742
Email: davidbrewster@freeola.com
www.thaxted.co.uk /morris.htm

SUFFOLK

Freston Tower, Freston
See Landmark Trust details on p154

Peter Pan House, Thorpeness
Aldeburgh Tourist Information
Tel/Fax: 01728 453637
www.suffolkcoastal.gov.uk

Ickworth House
The Rotunda, Horringer, Bury St Edmunds, Suffolk IP29 5QE
Tel: 01284 735270
Fax: 01284 735175
See National Trust details on p154

NORFOLK

Wymondham Abbey
The Abbey Office
Church Street, Wymondham
Norfolk NR18 0PH
Email:
wymondhamabbey@lineone.net
www.wymondham-norfolk.co.uk/abbey

Twinning Teapot Gallery
Norwich Castle, Castle Hill
Norwich, Norfolk NR13JU
Tel: 01603 493 625
Fax: 01603 493 623
Email: museums@norfolk.gov.uk
www.norfolk.gov.uk/tourism/museums

Helter-skelter House
Potter Heigham Tourist Information (open April–October)
Tel: 01692 670779

World Snail Racing Championships
Congham, Grimston, King's Lynn
Contact: Hilary Scase
Tel: 01485 600650
Fax: 01485 600672

HERTFORDSHIRE, BEDFORDSHIRE, BUCKINGHAMSHIRE, CAMBRIDGESHIRE & NORTHAMPTONSHIRE

BEDFORDSHIRE

Tree Cathedral, Whipsnade
c/o Chapel Farm, Whipsnade
Dunstable LU6 2LL
Tel: 01582 872406
See National Trust details on p154

Swiss Garden
Old Warden Park, Old Warden
Nr. Biggleswade SG18 9ER
Tel: 01767 626 236
Info Line Tel: 01767 627 666
www.bedfordshire.gov.uk

BUCKINGHAMSHIRE

Gothic Temple at Stowe Landscape Gardens
Stowe, Buckingham MK18 5EH
Tel: 01280 822850
Tel: 01280 822437
See National Trust and Landmark Trust details on p154

Hellfire Caves, West Wycombe
West Wycombe Caves Ltd.
Buckinghamshire HP14 3AJ
Tel: 01494 533739
Fax: 01494 471617
www.hellfirecaves.co.uk

CAMBRIDGESHIRE

Cheese-rolling Championship, Stilton
Tel: 01733 241206
www.stilton.org

Festival of Swans, Ouse Washes
The Wildfowl & Wetlands Trust
Hundred Foot Bank, Welney
Wisbech PE14 9TN
Tel: 01353 860711
Fax: 01353 860711
Email: info.welney@wwt.org.uk

Straw Bear Festival, Whittlesey
Tel: 01733 208245
Email: info@strawbear.org.uk
www.strawbear.org.uk

NORTHAMPTONSHIRE

Triangular Lodge
Rushton, Kettering NN14 1RP
Tel: 01536 710761 (open April–October)
See English Heritage details on p154

World Conker Championships, Ashton
Contact John Hadman
Tel: 01832 272735
Email:
john.hadman@btinternet.com

GLOUCESTERSHIRE, WARWICKSHIRE, HEREFORDSHIRE & WORCESTERSHIRE

GLOUCESTERSHIRE

Temple of Vaccinia
The Jenner Museum
The Chantry
Berkeley
Gloucestershire GL13 9BH
Tel: 01453 810631
Fax: 01453 811690
Email:
manager@jennermuseum.com
www.jennermuseum.com

Clypping Ceremony, St Mary's Church, Painswick
Painswick Tourist Office
Tel: 01452 813552

Cheese-rolling Competition Coopers Hill, Brockworth
Cheltenham Tourist Information
Tel: 01242 522878
Fax: 01242 255848

Sezincote House
Sezincote, Moreton-in-Marsh
Gloucestershire GL56 9AW
www.gardenvisit.com

Snowshill Manor
Snowshill
Broadway WR12 7JU
Tel: 01386 852410
Fax: 01386 842822
See National Trust details on p154

Olympick Games, Dover's Hill, Chipping Camden
Chipping Campden Tourist Information
Tel: 01386 841206

WARWICKSHIRE

Atherstone Ball Game, Atherstone
Contact Harold Taft
Tel: 01827 715786

HEREFORDSHIRE

Chain Library
Hereford Cathedral
5 College Cloisters
Cathedral Close
Hereford HR1 2NG
Tel: 01432 374200
Fax: 01432 374220
Email:
office@herefordcathedral.co.uk
www.herefordcathedral.co.uk

St Catherine's Church, Hoarwithy
Open all day

WORCESTERSHIRE

Broadway Tower
Broadway Tower Country Park
Middle Hill, Broadway
Worcestershire WR12 7LB
Tel: 01386 852390
Fax: 01386 858038

Hawford and Wichenford Dovecotes
See National Trust details on p154

Canal Locks, Tardebigge
Worcester Tourist Information
Tel: 01905 726311
Fax: 01905 722481

SHROPSHIRE, STAFFORDSHIRE, DERBYSHIRE, NOTTINGHAMSHIRE & LINCOLNSHIRE

SHROPSHIRE

Bridgnorth Castle
West Castle Street, Bridgnorth
Bridgnorth Tourist Information
Tel: 01746 763257

Ironbridge
The Ironbridge Gorge Museum
Coach Road, Coalbrookdale
Shropshire TF8 7DQ
Tel: 01952 884391
Fax: 01952 435999
Email: info@ironbridge.org.uk
www.ironbridge.org.uk

STAFFORDSHIRE

Gladstone Pottery Museum
Uttoxeter Road, Longton
Stoke-on-Trent ST3 1PQ
Tel: 01782 319232
Fax: 01782 598640
Email: gladstone@stoke.gov.uk
www2002.stoke.gov.uk/museums/gladstone

Abbots Bromley Horn Dance
Burton-on-Trent Tourist Information
Tel: 01283 508111
www.abbotsbromley.com

World Toe-wrestling Championship
Ye Olde Royal Oak pub
Wetton, Ashbourne
Derbyshire DE6 2AF
Tel: 01335 310287
Fax: 01335 310336

DERBYSHIRE

Eyam Village Museum
Hawkhill Road Eyam
Derbyshire S32 5QP
Tel/Fax: 01433 631371 (open 30th March–7th November)
www.eyammuseum.demon.co.uk

St Mary and All Saints' Church
Chesterfield Tourist Information
Tel: 01246 345777

NOTTINGHAMSHIRE

Mr Straw's House
7 Blyth Grove, Worksop S81 0JG
Tel: 01909 482380
See National Trust details on p154

LINCOLNSHIRE

Lincoln Imp
Lincoln Cathedral, LN2 1PZ
Tel: 01522 544544
www.lincolncathedral.com

Haxey Hood Game
http://members.lycos.co.uk/awheewall2/hood/hood.htm

CHESHIRE, LANCASHIRE, YORKSHIRE, CUMBRIA & DURHAM

CHESHIRE

Anderton Boat Lift
Lift Lane, Anderton
Northwich, Cheshire CW9 6FW
Tel: 01606 786777
Fax 01606 871471
Email: info@andertonboatlift.co.uk
www.andertonboatlift.co.uk

LANCASHIRE

Britannia Coco-nut Dancers
Email: info@coconutters.co.uk
www.coconutters.co.uk
Travellers Rest pub
Rochdale Road, Bacup OL13 9SD
Tel: 01706 873400

YORKSHIRE

World Coal-carrying Contest
The Royal Oak pub
Owl Lane, Gawthorpe, Ossett
West Yorkshire WF5 9AU
Tel: 01924 273965
www.gawthorpe.ndo.co.uk

Druid's Temple, llton
Thirsk Tourist Information
Tel: 01845 522755
www.herriotcountry.com

Tan Hill Inn
Keld, nr Richmond
North Yorkshire DL11 6ED
Tel: 01833 628246
www.tanhillinn.freewire.co.uk

Palladian Pigsty, Fyling
see Landmark Trust details on p154

Whitby Abbey, Yorkshire
Tel: 01947 603568
See English Heritage details on p154

CUMBRIA

Barrow Memorial Lighthouse
Hoad Hill, Ulverston
Ulverston Tourist Information
Tel: 01229 587120
Fax: 01229 582626

The Biggest Liar in the World Competition
The Bridge Inn, Santon Bridge
Wasdale, Cumbria CA19 1UX
Tel: 019467 26221
Fax: 019467 26026
Email: info@santonbridgeinn.com
www.santonbridgeinn.com/liar

Bridge House, Ambleside
St Catherine's, Patterdale Road
Windermere LA23 1NH
Tel: 015394 46027 / 32617
See National Trust details on p154

Egremont Crab Fair, Market Hall, Egremont
Egremont Tourist Information
Tel: 01946 820693

Bowder Stone, Grange, Borrowdale
National Trust Shop
Bowe Barn, Borrowdale Road
Keswick CA12 5UP
Tel: 017687 73780
See National Trust details on p154

DURHAM

Consett to Sunderland
Sustrans cycle track
Tel: 0845 113 0065
Email: info@sustrans.org.uk
www.sustrans.org.uk

Angel of the North, Gateshead
Gateshead Council
Tel: 0191 433 3000
www.gateshead.gov.uk/angel/index.html

WALES

Cardiff Castle
Castle Street, Cardiff CF10 3RB
Tel: 029 2087 8100
Fax: 029 2023 1417
Email: cardiffcastle@cardiff.gov.uk
www.cardiffcastle.com

Beating the Bounds, Laugharne
Carmarthenshire County Council
Tel: 01267 234567
www.carmarthenshire.gov.uk

World Bog Snorkelling Championships
Llanwrtyd Wells, Powys
Tel/Fax: 01591 610666
Email: lesley@celt.ruralwales.org
http://llanwrtyd-wells.powys.org.uk

Portmeirion
Porthmadog, Gwynedd LL48 6ET
Tel: 01766 770228
Fax: 01766 771331
Email: enquiries@portmeirion-village.com
www.portmeirion-village.com

Snowdon Mountain Railway
Llanberis, Gwynedd LL55 4TY
Tel: 01286 870223
Fax: 01286 872518

Plas Newydd and the Marquess of Anglesey's Leg
Llanfairpwll LL61 6DQ
Tel: 01248 715272
Fax: 01248 713673
See National Trust details on p154

Plas Newydd, Llangollen
Tel: 01978 861314
Llangollen Tourist Information
Tel: 01978 860 828
Fax: 01978 861928

SCOTLAND

Hawick & Selkirk Common Riding
Scottish Borders Tourist Board
Tel: 01750 720054
www.visitscottishborders.com

Robert the Bruce's heart
Melrose Abbey, Abbey Street,
Melrose, Roxburghshire TD6 9LG
Tel: 01896 822 562
www.historic-scotland.gov.uk

Greyfriars Bobby, Edinburgh
Bobby's monument is on the corner of Candlemakers Row and King George IV Bridge; Bobby's grave is inside Greyfriars Kirkyard.
www.greyfriarsbobby.co.uk

Pineapple House
Dunmore Park, Stirlingshire
See the Landmark Trust and National Trust for Scotland details on p154

South Queensferry Burry Man
Queensferry Museum
Tel: 0131 331 5545
Fax: 0131 557 3346
www.edinburgh.gov.uk

McCaig's folly, Oban
Oban Tourist Information
Tel: 01631 563122,
Fax: 01631 564273
www.oban.org.uk

Highland Games, Braemar
Braemar Tourist Information
Tel: 013397 41600

Burning of the Clavie, Burghead
Elgin Tourist Information
Tel: 01463 234353
Fax: 01343 542666
www.aberdeen-grampian.com

Up Helly Aa, Lerwick
Shetland Islands Tourism
Tel: 01595 693434
Fax: 01595 695807
www.visitshetland.com

Index

Primary references are in **bold**. Page numbers in *italics* refer to illustrations.

Acknowledgements

Des Hannigan thanks his many eccentric friends and associates (they do not know who they are) who have inspired him over the years and whose attitudes and behaviour are often mirrored in the eccentricities featured in this book. Great thanks to Tim Hannigan and Martin Dunning for their advice, input and wit, on more practical matters. A very big thank you to Camilla MacWhannell at New Holland for her patient steering of the project through reefs of eccentricity. Thanks also to Jo Hemmings and Kate Michell for launching the concept; to Alan Marshall and Gülen Shevki for their fine design work and to William Smuts for mapping. Special thanks to Chris Coe for lighting up the pages with pictures and to Miren Lopategui for lucid editing of my often anarchic copy.

Finally, my enduring gratitude to the many Historical and Heritage organisations, academics, librarians (especially the marvellous and highly professional staff of Penzance Public Library), tourism officers, local experts and outrageous gossips with whom I have worked during many years of research and writing about Britain – that *ultima thule* of fascinating diversity and quirkiness. The centre will always hold, so long as eccentricity thrives.

Photographic Credits

The Dean and Chapter of Hereford and the Hereford Mappa Mundi Trust: p101

Edifice/Darley: p86

Gladstone Pottery Museum, Stoke-on-Trent: p108

The Jenner Museum: p96

Sir John Soane's Museum/Martin Charles: p68

The Landmark Trust: p77 (Nicolette Hallett); p145 (Nigel Shuttleworth)

Mary Evans Picture Library: p30 (Douglas McCarthy); p60 (Harry Price); p151 (Hugh Gray)

Mike McKenzie: p127

Phil Monckton: p12

Eric A Roy: p109

Somerset Archaeological and History Society: p32

www.ShetlandTourism.Com: p153